Alas, Poor Uranus

Sci-Fi & Fantasy for the Stage

Brent Winzek

with Zachary Gold

Space Cadets Studios

Edited by C.J. Barrett

Cover art by Monica Kay

For more, visit spacecadetsstudios.com

ISBN: 979-8-9885955-6-4

DEDICATION

To Dr. Michael Ellison for his otherworldly inspiration &
to all the artists who first brought these shorts to life.
In loving memory of Dr. Darin Kerr.

ACKNOWLEDGMENTS

Both writers owe special thanks to the keen eyes of editor C.J. Barrett, and to test readers Joe Connelly, Wes Gilbert, Kyle Petitjean, & Monica Kay. The enclosed scenes would not have their current shape and structure without the hard work and dedication of the thespians who first staged them around Bowling Green, Ohio between the years 2006 – 2012.

Author Brent Winzek would like to acknowledge the extra efforts and enthusiasm of his protégé and friend Zack Gold for his ever-honest feedback with revisions and his diligence in curating this collection. Further gratitude is due to college cohort, contemporary colleague, & good friend Chase Will for his loyal literary endorsements since the days when these scripts were first written. Finally, these plays simply would not have been reworked if Brent's wife & family hadn't encouraged all his strange writing habits from the very start.

Co-author Zachary Gold would like to acknowledge his mentor and friend Brent Winzek for bringing him onboard as part of this exciting project. Zack would also like to extend thanks to his parents, friends & family for their continued support in his artistic endeavors.

CONCEPTUAL STATEMENT

When I brought this project to Zack for help assembling it, my primary goal was simple: neither of us had encountered very much science fiction in our time studying theater. As huge fans of the genre, it's something we both lamented throughout our undergraduate theater pursuits.

With my own backlog of short, silly plays, I envisioned a script that could function in short presentations or in continuity as one production. From that concept, Zack and I developed the interstitial 'Executive Decisions' sequence. Those snippets serve two purposes. For one, they string together these otherwise disparate scenes so that the whole script has a sense of cohesion, start-to-finish, like a sketch comedy variety show. Secondly, we each found ourselves moved to offer commentary on the creative struggles faced by contemporary writers in the science fiction genre in a post-*Star Wars* era of popular culture.

The theatrically inclined reader is encouraged to single out a scene for individual workshops or performances. To make all scenes accessible, we have included a continuous version of the 'Executive Decisions' script at the back of the book.

-Brent Winzek

PERFORMANCE RIGHTS

STAGE DIRECTIONS

Many of the descriptions within these scripts suggest spectacle and may therefore seem outlandish or impractical to produce. The creative team need only capture their essence.

For changes to a character's gender, adjust pronouns as needed.

CONTENTS

EXECUTIVE DECISIONS I

CAST:

GEORGE – (M) 60s, overweight with white hair & beard.

BEAU BASIC – (M or F) 50s, uptight but smart producer in their own head.

JAX WEISSMAN – (M) 30s or 40s, cut–throat, fast-talking producer.

PRODUCTION NOTES:

Executive Decisions can be performed in parts, as presented here, or as one continuous, independent One Act, as presented at the back of the book.

LIGHTS UP

A mid-1990s corporate Hollywood conference room sits empty apart from GEORGE, *who wears a plaid flannel shirt tucked into his jeans. He sits at the end of the conference table, shuffling script pages, peering at them through tiny glasses perched at the end of his nose.*

He puts the pages down and pulls out two miniature spaceships, holding them up at different angles as if his eye were a camera lens.

JAX WEISSMAN *and* BEAU BASIC *burst through the conference room's double doors, or fly in from the rafters, landing on the table like it's a helipad.*

JAX: Sorry we're late, George. Completely my fault. Well, between us three, I blame the bitch I've got on my latest project.

GEORGE: Oh. (*shaking his head*) I'm sorry, please don't use that term.

JAX: Are you– ? (*turning to Beau*) Is he serious? (*back to George*) Are you fuckin' serious?

GEORGE: I–

JAX: Remind me, was it your movie that gave Carrie an eating disorder? Know, because you insisted on putting her in a metal bikini for nearly five minutes of screen time.

GEORGE: It's un–

JAX: Did you know that Beau here got his start producing pornos, eh? Did you know that?

GEORGE: No, but–

JAX: How long's your average porn, Beau?

BEAU: Anywhere from ten minutes to two hours. But we find that most men usually focus on no more than three minutes of screen time.

JAX: (*nodding triumphantly*) Bang. That's what I was looking for. Thank you, Beau. (*to George*) Ya' hear that, Grandpa Feminism? You made that poor girl wear that thing for more screen time than your average crank–yanker.

GEORGE: (*defeated*) No one's ever pointed that out before…

JAX: (*beat*) Also, because I feel attacked, I should point out that I was referring to an actual female dog, so fuck you, times two. (*snapping back to a pleasant smile*) That was fun. I mean, I was excited to meet with you anyway, but that was just exhilarating, George!

GEORGE: I, uh–

JAX: I should tell you I'm not fucking with you right now. Things are going to get vicious– this is a negotiation, after all. We have to be able to speak freely and (*he closes his eyes, breathes deep, and pushes his arms out as he exhales*) acknowledge and release the tension. Feel free to say whatever you need to say to me, too, George. I mean that.

BEAU: (*meekly*) He does, yeah.

GEORGE: Thank… you?

JAX: (*smiling*) Have I said it's good to see you again?

GEORGE: Uh–

JAX: Since we're all in good spirits, let's dive right in. Loving the storyboards, really, but there is a major concern with the big climax.

GEORGE: Oh?

BEAU: Yes, uh, according to one of our script analysts, there's an alarming number of scenes using tumbling, falling, and heights in some manner. We're concerned–

JAX: The investors are concerned, Beau. We love it. Don't we, Beau?

BEAU: Yes? Yes. The *investors* are concerned...

JAX: ...that we'll upset people with agoraphobia.

BEAU: Are you saying that right?

JAX: Yeah, that's what my notes say. I keep very detailed notes.

Pushing up his sleeve, Jax extends his left arm and squints at the palm and wrist of that hand. After a beat, Beau clears his throat gently.

BEAU: My memo says 'acrophobia: fear of heights.'

JAX: Tomayto, tomahto. Point is, we don't want so many scenes with people falling and flipping and every other damned thing. It's unsettling and, frankly, not very believable after the first watch.

GEORGE: These characters don't really fall; they tumble and double jump with their Force powers… think of it more like acrobatics?

JAX: Oh, and it works for the wizards with laser swords. Don't change a thing, there. We want to leave those acrobatics, but trim back in other instances. For example, the investors think you should cut this fifth storyline in your climax where your rabbit-frog Jar-Jar goes into the swamps to fight a boss droid on his own. You've already got enough going on, and that eliminates your literal cliffhanger. If you agree to that, then we're in business!

GEORGE: *(to self)* Cut the fifth storyline… that would streamline a few things… *(to Jax)* Yeah, sure. I mean, I'm sacrificing artistic vision here, but I could make that work.

BLACKOUT.

TRAVELERS ON THE FIRE ESCAPE

CAST:

TAYLOR – (M, F or NB) 30s or 40s. Clean–cut, professional & skittish.
ASTRONAUT – (F or NB) Older than Taylor.
COACHMAKER – (M) Younger than Taylor.

LIGHTS UP

A worn red fire escape groans in the wind stage right. It shares a wall with the living room of a small New York City apartment.

The room is neat and orderly, all furniture squared and centered along the wall. A couch and chair take up most of the space. A small TV sits opposite the couch, and a flimsy card table sits under the windows.

An exit upstage clearly leads to the kitchen. Somewhere in that vicinity, a coffeemaker sputters.

An alarm clock chirps, cut off by a thump off left.

TAYLOR, *a clean–cut Poindexter–type, enters from left. He shuffles across the hardwood floor, his plain blue bathrobe swaying.*

He places a coffee mug and a plate with buttered toast on the flimsy card table and sits facing the window.

Methodically, Taylor nibbles at the toast, then plucks a small piece off and dunks it in his coffee. This is clearly a ritual.

A brilliant white light pulsates and electricity crackles. A fog rolls in from off right.

Thunder roars. Taylor jolts, dropping his toast into his coffee.

TAYLOR: (*muttering*) What in the…

Trembling, he stands, then whips the curtains open and peers outside.

The fire escape rattles and moans as the ASTRONAUT, *a woman wearing a shimmering silver jumpsuit, hustles down its metal stairs.*

Taylor ducks behind his curtains, peeking timidly.

Behind the Astronaut, the COACHMAKER, *follows. He sports dirty pantaloons, a poet blouse with billowy sleeves, and a tricorn hat.*

They stop on the fire escape outside Taylor's window and survey the city beyond.

COACHMAKER: Twenty-first century New York.

ASTRONAUT: Yep… at the end of its better days, too.

COACHMAKER: Oh?

Hiding by the window, Taylor shifts, bumping his foot on the card table leg. The whole table shifts.

The Coachmaker turns, spying Taylor through the curtains.

COACHMAKER: Begging your pardon, sir?

Taylor freezes, tangled in his curtains.

COACHMAKER: Rest assured, sir, I am addressing you: the man behind the curtain.

Taylor frantically draws the curtains. Fumbling, he pinches at the toast inside his coffee mug. He retrieves it, sets it on his plate and frowns, then scoops up his breakfast and clears it, crossing towards his kitchen.

Before he can exit, the Astronaut raps on the window.

ASTRONAUT: Hey– we know you're in there!

TAYLOR: No, I'm not!

Taylor startles himself, clasping his hand over his mouth. He exits, setting the dishes down with a clink.

The knocking continues as Taylor re-enters, shuffling his feet as he sips his coffee. He stands as far from the window as possible, staring intently at various things on the opposite side of the apartment.

The Astronaut keeps knocking. Taylor plugs one ear with his finger.

The knocking continues. Taylor hums a bit of Mozart.

The knocking persists. Taylor clenches his fists, stands, and marches to the window. He throws open the curtains.

TAYLOR: Leave me alone! Go bother someone else.

Taylor whips the curtains closed again.

COACHMAKER: Why?

TAYLOR: Because I don't like being bothered!

ASTRONAUT: We need to see you.

Taylor takes a beat, then whips the curtain open again.

TAYLOR: Why me?

COACHMAKER: Something you're going to do.

TAYLOR: (*laughing*) Something I'm *going to do*, huh? Sure. Sure!

COACHMAKER: Taylor Williams, where are your manners, boy? Can you not see us both standing here in the cold of winter while you deliberate?

TAYLOR: Hey, *guy*, I don't know where the hell you're from–

ASTRONAUT: *When* we're from–

TAYLOR: –but in New York, when assholes show up on your fire escape in the dead of winter using your name and asking to come in, it's not exactly common practice to go along with the delusion.

ASTRONAUT: (*shaking her head*) I know it sounds crazy… *he* especially sounds crazy (*she points to the Coachmaker*), but at least hear us out?

TAYLOR: I should warn you, if this is some hidden camera show bullshit, I want no part in it. I have friends who work in TV. I know you need me to sign a release, and I'll tell you right now I won't do it! No way; absolutely n– !

ASTRONAUT: I'm not on a hidden camera show. I won't technically be born for another five hundred years.

Taylor raises an eyebrow at the Coachmaker, who tips his hat.

COACHMAKER: And I, the year of our Lord seventeen hundred and sixty–three.

TAYLOR: (*chews on his lip a moment*) What are you? Actors?

COACHMAKER: Heavens, no! How dreadful!

ASTRONAUT: Our only concern is you.

TAYLOR: Uh, oh… okay. And you want what, exactly?

ASTRONAUT: A glass of water and somewhere to sit, for starters.

TAYLOR: No.

COACHMAKER: Oh, come off it. Make the more interesting decision! If you could possibly manage before we freeze through, that would be splendid.

Taylor glares, but, after a moment of thought, he grabs an aluminum baseball bat from behind the door, raising it awkwardly as he approaches. He unlatches the window and lets the strangers in.

As they climb inside, Taylor raises the baseball bat, demonstrating that he is armed. He gestures to the sofa.

The Astronaut and Coachmaker raise their hands as if regarding someone armed with a gun, then shuffle over to sit on the couch.

TAYLOR: Don't move! Stay right where you are, or so help me–

Taylor works his arms, as if warming up with the baseball bat. Then, he exits quickly.

A moment later, he re-enters with the baseball bat and a pitcher of coffee.

TAYLOR: Toast'll be ready in just a few minutes.

Taylor pauses, looking down at the coffee table.

TAYLOR: Shoot, wait.

Taylor rushes out, still holding the pitcher of coffee and baseball bat.

He returns quickly with two clean, plain mugs and a potholder. He throws the potholder onto the coffee table, exits to the kitchen, then returns with the coffee pitcher and the baseball bat.

Taylor pours his guests each a mug of steaming coffee, then sets the hot pitcher on the potholder. He does all of this methodically, then rushes back to the kitchen.

Offstage, a toaster oven dings, and Taylor returns with a plate of toast stacked twelve (or more) slices high. He sets it on the table.

TAYLOR: Coffee on an empty stomach always gives me heartburn. Toast helps.

The Astronaut plucks a slice of toast off the stack and butters it.

ASTRONAUT: Should we be alarmed by your sudden cooperation?

Taylor refills his coffee, then sits at his card table, staring at them from across the room. He lays the baseball bat across his lap.

TAYLOR: Would you like jelly?

ASTRONAUT: Nah.

COACHMAKER: No, thank you.

TAYLOR: So, do you have names, or...?

COACHMAKER: I'm the Coachmaker; she's the Astronaut.

TAYLOR: Those are titles, really.

ASTRONAUT: We don't use names. It's dangerous.

Taylor feigns understanding and takes a sip of his coffee.

TAYLOR: (*studies the Coachmaker, then…*) Doesn't any of this shock you?

COACHMAKER: Are you referring to the television?

TAYLOR: Among other things.

COACHMAKER: I have traveled with the Astronaut for quite some time. I am a learn'ed man.

TAYLOR: How long?

COACHMAKER: I have not counted the years. They are… conceptual from where we sit.

TAYLOR: Years?

ASTRONAUT: (*shrugging*) It's what I do. But years can pass like hours the way we travel.

The Coachmaker chuckles along with this, then, growing severe, turns to Taylor.

COACHMAKER: Tell me, Taylor Williams, are you not the least bit interested in what we want with you?

TAYLOR: You mean apart from forcible entry and free toast?

ASTRONAUT: God, you're thick.

COACHMAKER: I do thank ye' for the toast.

Taylor taps the brim of his mug.

TAYLOR: (*through clenched teeth*) Why are you here?

ASTRONAUT: You don't get out much.

TAYLOR: Work. I work. Quite a bit, in fact.

The Astronaut stares at Taylor as she extracts another piece of toast from the plate in front of her.

ASTRONAUT: We think you should come with us.

TAYLOR: I have a job. I have obligations.

ASTRONAUT: They'll be here. Right when you left them.

TAYLOR: Oh, great! Sure! And where, exactly, are you going?

COACHMAKER: When.

TAYLOR: What?

COACHMAKER: *When* are we going.

ASTRONAUT: We could use the company.

TAYLOR: Look, I only let you in so you'd go away.

ASTRONAUT: (*under her breath*) Flawed logic, that.

TAYLOR: I've given you toast– I used the last of my coffee– I had enough to last 'til grocery day, but now I'll wake up tomorrow with no coffee. So, there's that. Thank you very much!

The Astronaut grabs her mug from the coffee table and crosses to Taylor, who clenches his eyes shut, cowering. She pours her mug of coffee into his, and he opens his eyes.

TAYLOR: What are you doing? Stop it!

The mug overflows and coffee slops onto the floor. The Astronaut waits as the last drop drips into Taylor's mug, her eyes locked with his.

ASTRONAUT No. I *refuse* to be an inconvenience.

TAYLOR: You're only making it worse!

Taylor's hands tremble as he tries to suck down the coffee in his overflowing mug.

COACHMAKER: You seem uneasy, Mr. Williams.

TAYLOR: (*getting worked up, possibly to tears*) Of course I'm uneasy! I brought two nutjobs in out of the cold and my morning routine is shot to pieces! This is exactly what my psychiatrist meant when she said I have no boundaries!

ASTRONAUT: Come with us. Do something with yourself.

TAYLOR: I thought you wanted toast!

COACHMAKER: No. We want you.

TAYLOR: Why?

ASTRONAUT: We can't tell you until you've chosen.

TAYLOR: I don't understand.

ASTRONAUT: You don't have to.

COACHMAKER: Taylor, what we are driving at here is a leap of faith.

ASTRONAUT: I thought I got to say that part!

COACHMAKER: You had yet to come to it, my dear. The poor boy is all out of sorts as it is. Recall, if you will, how our own paths came to cross.

ASTRONAUT: Fine… *fine.* (*to Taylor*) We can't tell you what we need until you've chosen to come with us.

COACHMAKER: Of your own free–

ASTRNOAUT: Free will. Yeah, I got it, thank you. (*to Taylor*) You have to choose to come with us of your own free will.

TAYLOR: Oh. Kay. Okay. Uh… and, um… what– uh, how… no.

ASTRONAUT: I don't follow the question.

TAYLOR: Yeah, there isn't one yet because I don't know what to ask. Give me a second, thanks.

The Astronaut and Coachmaker recoil, their eyes going wide at Taylor's tone. They sit awkwardly, unwilling to speak.

TAYLOR: Well… I guess… I suppose the question I have is: This thing you can't tell me until I choose to join you; is it important? Does the very fabric of existence hang in the balance, or something?

ASTRONAUT: What?

COACHMAKER: Goodness, no! Nothing so terrible.

ASTRONAUT: If that were true, we wouldn't be here. I mean, what the hell are we gonna do about that? We're not quantum physicists, for Chris' sake. More like system defraggers, really.

TAYLOR: Then no. My answer is, 'No.'

COACHMAKER: How about the fabric of your own existence, you Lollpoop prig?

Taylor shrinks in his seat.

ASTRONAUT: Language.

COACHMAKER: Apologies.

Taylor's stomach gurgles audibly, propelling him suddenly from his seat.

TAYLOR: Excuse me. Confrontation works up my anxiety, and I've already had coffee. I just– I'll be right back.

Taylor rushes off left. A door shuts, a fan hums to life, and a toilet seat clanks violently.

COACHMAKER: This boy is infuriating!

ASTRONAUT: Easy. Don't get your knickers in a twist.

COACHMAKER: My knickers *cannot* twist, damn you! (*catching himself*) Apologies. I do not know what seizes me so.

ASTRONAUT: You getting a little hangry?

COACHMAKER: What in God's name– ?

ASTRONAUT: C'mon. Let's leave him to it. With how long he takes with decisions, we can grab food downtown *and* eat it before he hits our rendezvous timeline.

COACHMAKER: Could we not simply travel back with more time to spare?

ASTRONAUT: Now you're thinking four-dimensionally!

The Astronaut plucks a small red device from her pocket. She sets it on the card table, next to Taylor's baseball bat, and presses a sticky note to the device.

ASTRONAUT: C'mon, let's blow this popsicle stand.

They cross back to the window together, hopping out onto the fire escape.

COACHMAKER: I have not the slightest idea what you just said.

ASTRONAUT: (*shrugging*) I'm a fan of this era. I've been here for R 'n' R a few times.

They climb the fire escape, exiting up out of sight. The window to Taylor's apartment is left wide open, and his curtains flutter in the wind.

Taylor rushes back into the room.

TAYLOR: Sorry about that, I– guys? Hello?

In the middle of his empty living room, Taylor spins, looking around. He spots the small red device on the card table and snatches the sticky note attached to it.

TAYLOR: (*reading*) "One: Hold device firmly. Two: Climb fire escape. Three: Fall... backwards."

Taylor rolls his eyes and crumples up the sticky note.

A flash of light and rumble of thunder erupt from outside.

The bright light fades as Taylor rushes to the open window. Apart from the howling winter wind and the drone of city traffic, all is still. Silent.

TAYLOR: (*quietly to self*) Fuck me…

Noticing the tower of toast, Taylor grabs a half–eaten slice placed neatly on top of the stack. With a frown, he takes a bite. He stares at the palm-sized red device as he chews, then surveys his surroundings.

Taylor sighs, grabbing the red device. He climbs out the window.

Taylor stares at the metal staircase.

TAYLOR: Fuck *me*.

BLACKOUT

END.

EXECUTIVE DECISIONS II

LIGHTS UP

JAX *drums his fingers on the table. He does not speak, just studies* GEORGE.

BEAU *lingers quietly in a corner.*

GEORGE: Is there something else?

Jax continues drumming his fingers.

JAX: Yeah, but… well, to be honest, I'm still not certain it's an issue. It may just be a 'me' thing, okay?

GEORGE: Uh, yeah, sure. Okay. What, um… what's the–

Seized by dramatic compulsion, Jax smacks the table with both fists.

JAX: There's no *Chew*bacca, George!

George jolts back with a start.

Beau chokes on his bottled water.

GEORGE: Well, uh, no… that's right, there's not.

JAX: Why the fuck not, George?

BEAU: Gotta say, I missed Chewbacca, too. Yeah.

JAX: I think it's a really weak choice. I mean, you've got kid-Vader, kid-Greedo, undergrad Obi-wan and even notes about a shiny Falcon cameo.

GEORGE: How did you like all that?

JAX: I liked it better when I thought we were going to meet teenage mutant ninja Chewbacca in the sewers of your pollution planet or something!

GEORGE: Pollution planet?

BEAU: The dirty city planet that's always gray and gloomy?

GEORGE: That's Coruscant. The entire planet's a city and–

JAX: Nobody cares! You know why?

GEORGE: (*quietly, defeated*) No Chewbacca?

JAX: No Chewbacca! I nearly wept. I do not weep, George. Except for *Schindler's List.* Phenomenal accomplishment. If you don't cry, you're a monster.

George shifts in his chair.

JAX: Here's the thing: the investors ran the numbers, and Chewbacca ticks a lot of boxes in the crowd-pleaser Coliseum. Beau, do you have that printout?

BEAU: Yes, here!

Beau plucks a sheet of paper from a snack counter in the corner of the conference room.

BEAU: According to focus groups, Chewbacca scores higher in onscreen audience appeal than cinema's most popular animal stars.

JAX: I know the significance of this won't be lost on you, George. Like W. C. Fields said, "Never work with children or animals." Those bastards will upstage anyone!

BEAU: In these crowd preference surveys, Chewbacca rates five times higher than toy dogs like Shi-Tzus, three times higher than large dogs like Huskies or Lassie, and– here's the kicker– twice as high as large mammals, like a bear or a lion.

GEORGE: Wow, I… actually, I didn't know that. Can I have a copy of that?

JAX: I'm afraid it's confidential company research. But for the purposes of this meeting, I can let you look at it. Beau?

Beau holds the paper out. George adjusts his glasses, squinting as he reads the numbers.

JAX: Knowing this, just think what a money-maker that goofy Christmas Special would've–

GEORGE: (*loud and upset, like a child*) Strike one!

JAX: What– ?

BEAU: Uh– oh! Jax, you broke his only rule.

JAX: I'm sorry, George. I got carried away with myself. Honestly, I know we aren't supposed to mention… *it*… but you should know that I liked *it* a lot as a kid. Truly.

GEORGE: I'm only counting that as one, but you'd better tread lightly. (*he holds up two fingers, like an umpire*) Two more strikes and I'm out!

BEAU: I think what Jax was trying to express before he derailed himself there is that we wanted Wookies. Instead of Naboo and these weird Gung-hos–

GEORGE: You mean Gungans.

BEAU: Right. Well, instead of them, why not use the Wookies and take us to their home world?

GEORGE: Kashyyk?

BEAU: Sure. If that's what you call it.

GEORGE: I hadn't thought of that.

JAX: Everyone loves Chewbacca, George. He's like the Star Wars sasquatch! Brilliant crowd appeal. I mean that from the heart.

BLACKOUT.

CRYPTID COUNSELING

CAST:

EMMA – (F) 30s or 40s. Rugged, but in that 'overconfident suburbanite' way. The tough yoga instructor.

CRAIG – (M) 30s or 40s. A simple man bored with life and getting more selfish with age.

SASQUATCH – (M) Any age… a gentleman with a pervading wisdom, Renaissance charm, and a voice like John Cleese.

DEBUT PRODUCTION CREDITS:

Produced & performed for Theta Alpha Phi's Shortsfest 2009 *in Bowling Green, Ohio with the following artists:*

Director: C.J. Barrett
Emma: Eli Brickey
Craig: Joe Connelly
Sasquatch: Scott Stechschulte
Costuming: Kimberly Yehoda–Barrett

SCENE 1

LIGHTS UP

A sprawling forest of evergreens somewhere in the North American West. The forest floor glows golden–green as sunlight leaks through the tall trees, spackling the ground.

Birds chirp and crickets hum. A creek babbles nearby.

The peace is interrupted by distant bickering voices…

EMMA: (*offstage*) Oh, no. You always tell me *how it is.* It's my turn!

CRAIG: (*sarcastically*) Oh, you're right. You're absolutely right. I've never once, in seven years together, ever admitted when I was wrong.

EMMA *trudges in from stage left, talking over her shoulder. She is fit and determined, outfitted like a Patagonia print ad.*

Behind her, CRAIG *barrels in. He is rotund but fit, though his casual shorts and wrinkled graphic* Looney Tunes *T-shirt don't necessarily showcase his physique.*

EMMA: You're oh–for–four today! You were wrong about following the creek and you were wrong about which way was north. You were wrong about which side of the rock that moss was growing on, and you were wrong five minutes ago when you said we weren't going in circles because there's my fucking hair tie, hanging from that branch I looped it on when we passed through here the first time!

CRAIG: Okay, fine! Yes! Clearly, that's your hair tie, which means *yes,* we went in a circle *this last* time. I was wrong. Okay? But, and I'm just putting this out there, is it also my fault you didn't pack enough water and snacks? Silly me, I fucked everything up! Is that what you're saying?

Craig sniffs the air over the creek as Emma talks. He smiles, kneels, and cups his hands, scooping up some babbling creek water.

EMMA: Yes, Craig, yes, it is. That's exactly what I'm saying. I'm blaming all of my problems on you. It's your fault I wanted to try doing something together. It's your fault I'm trying to salvage what's left of our relationship.

CRAIG: (*to himself in a soprano voice*) It's your fault I broke a nail. It's your fault I love you. It's your fault my dad was an alcoholic.

EMMA: Craig! Seriously? This is exactly what Dr. Carlson was talking about. Stop mocking me. I'm trying here!

CRAIG: I know, I just… I think you're trying too hard, okay? It's like Coyote and Roadrunner, y'know?

EMMA: No– please tell me how and why you compare our relationship to *Looney Tunes.*

CRAIG: When you spin it like that, it sounds awful. What I meant was maybe we're trying too hard. Coyote never caught the stupid Roadrunner because he was always overthinking things. Right? And Roadrunner, she just *lives–*

EMMA: Hold on, you think Roadrunner's a girl?

CRAIG: Yeah… the eyelashes?

Emma nods approvingly.

EMMA: Go on…

CRAIG: Well, Roadrunner, she's just a free spirit. She doesn't think about it, so she gets away. Coyote, on the other hand, uses all kinds of unnatural gadgetry to catch his prey. Meanwhile, he's a predator, and all he really needs to do is get his claws dirty. Maybe our relationship is like that right now? We're overthinking it with the therapy and these planned outings– the gadgetry– when all we really need is to focus on being us.

EMMA: (*she nods slowly, processing*) Okay. That's… very thoughtful and definitely more nuanced than I was expecting. I'm sorry for being cynical about your comparison.

CRAIG: Thank you.

Craig doubles over, wincing.

EMMA: Craig? Hon? (s*he shakes him gently*) Hey, c'mon. Get up.

Craig groans, doubling over in pain.

CRAIG: (*through the pain*) My gut…

EMMA: I think you're dehydrated. We need to get you back.

CRAIG: (*not coherent*) Why *didn't* Coyote ever catch the Roadrunner?

EMMA: What?

CRAIG: I mean, I know that's the joke, but you always follow Wile E. Coyote as if he's the protagonist. But he always gets his ass beat by the roadrunner. That doesn't seem right. Don't coyotes *eat* roadrunners in the wild?

EMMA: The metaphor's falling apart, babe. You're talking gibberish. C'mon, get up. We should get you out of here.

CRAIG: (*through the pain*) Uh huh. Agreed. I need a toilet.

As Emma helps Craig up, an exceptionally short Sasquatch enters, dancing with earbuds in as he swipes at his phone screen, not noticing the couple. He wears a silk cravat and elegant smoking jacket.

Craig spots him and points.

CRAIG: (*completely out of it*) Look, it's Wile E. Coyote! Helloooo, Mr. Coyote!

Sasquatch looks up, sees them, and freezes.

SASQUATCH: Oh, hell.

EMMA: Stop it, Craig. Go squat in a bush or something.

Emma shoos Craig upstage. He disappears behind a tree.

Sasquatch turns to leave quietly, but Emma pivots, finally spotting him.

EMMA: Hey!

Sasquatch freezes mid–step and turns to face them, striking the classic 'Bigfoot' pose.

SASQUATCH: (*to himself*) Heh. Oh, bugger. (*to Emma*) Hello! What brings you to... (*long, awkward pause*) this neck of the woods?

EMMA: You can talk?

SASQUATCH: Um, yes.

EMMA: You're Bigfoot.

SASQUATCH: Well, Sasquatch, but yes.

EMMA: Sasquatch, Bigfoot; same thing.

SASQUATCH: Not really.

EMMA: Huh?

SASQUATCH: Never you mind.

EMMA: You're not very… uh, big.

SASQUATCH: Right. Which is why 'Bigfoot' is a bit of a misnomer… and silly. Quite silly. My feet are by no means big, especially considering average foot-to-body proportions.

EMMA: (*utterly confounded*) Am I hallucinating?

SASQUATCH: Umm... yes?

CRAIG: (*off*) Say 'hi' to Wile E. Coyote for me, Emma. Is he still there?

EMMA: (*calling to Craig*) Yeah, hon', he's still here. (*quietly to Sasquatch*) I'm not crazy. He can see you, too. He thinks you're Wile E. Coyote, but he saw you.

SASQUATCH: Look I'm just gonna keep moving. You're not supposed to get to see me. So, I'll just be on my way.

EMMA: Wait, wait, wait! Do you know which way I need to go to get back to the ranger station?

SASQUATCH: Yes, but I really shouldn't be with you out here.

EMMA: If you don't help us, we're probably gonna die, so…

Craig returns, kneeling next to the creek. He scoops the water up in his hands and drinks it.

SASQUATCH: No offense, but you wouldn't be the first and you probably won't be the last. But hey, good luck and it was nice meeting you (*shaking Emma's hand*). Don't drink the creek water, there's a high risk of E. coli and Legionella. Cheers!

Craig leans over and drinks from the creek again.

Sasquatch turns to leave, but Emma lets out a yell and tackles him to the ground.

SASQUATCH: Ow!

Emma adjusts her hold on Sasquatch, locking him in a half-nelson. Then, she starts to squeeze. During this, Craig stands, feels better, then doubles over again.

EMMA: Look, man, I don't want to hurt you, but I'm getting desperate here. This was supposed to be a therapy exercise, and it is *not* working. What's worse, he hates it *and* he's being intolerable, and now he's not feeling well. Probably because he's been drinking the creek water all day. So now, he's going to be a *child* about everything for the rest of the day. If you don't lead us back, I'm gonna snap your neck and drag your body back so I can sell it for scientific experiments. Don't think I won't!

SASQUATCH: Could– could you not squeeze *so* hard?

EMMA: Answer me!

SASQUATCH: I don't have much choice, do I? (*a beat as he struggles*) Fine, I'll help, but if I do, you can't tell anyone you saw me, and you can't hurt me. Deal?

EMMA: Deal.

She releases him. Together, they help Craig to his feet. Craig seems woozy with illness as he processes the world around him in slow motion. The pain in his gut persists.

CRAIG: Oh, hey… you're not Mr. Coyote. Your face is too flat.

Craig boops Sasquatch on the nose. Sasquatch swats his hand away.

They all exit together.

BLACKOUT.

SCENE 2

LIGHTS UP

The three enter from stage right, still biking.

Craig is with it but still leaning on Emma and wincing in abdominal pain.

CRAIG: (*to Emma*) I just don't know if it's a good idea to trust him.

EMMA: Well, what would you suggest? At least he knows his way around the forest, which is more than I can say for you.

CRAIG: Oh, don't start this again. There was something funky about that map they gave us. I've studied map reading.

EMMA: When? When have you ever studied map reading?

CRAIG: I earned my cartography badge when I was in Boy Scouts.

Ahead of them, Sasquatch cackles, scoffing.

CRAIG: What's so goddamn funny?

SASQUATCH: I just don't think having a Boy Scout badge constitutes the claim that you "studied cartography."

EMMA: (*to Craig*) See? I've told you before you embellish things.

SASQUATCH: (*sitting down*) It's also a perfect example of wielding knowledge and experience for self-validation. Perhaps because you feel that, based on where you're at in life, you didn't reach your full potential? That you didn't try hard enough? And perhaps that also puts a strain on your relationship?

CRAIG: What, are you Sigmund Freud now? Am I paying for a psychiatrist? If I want your opinion, I'll ask for it. Besides, where the hell do you get off trying to teach me people skills, Chewbacca?

SASQUATCH: And yet you're the one whose vocabulary seems limited to barks and growls.

EMMA: Craig! Don't insult him. He's trying to help us.

CRAIG: You. He was helping *you* by picking on *me.* That's not helping us, that's just taking your side.

EMMA: There you go deflecting again. Maybe he has a point?

CRAIG: Oh, don't start.

SASQUATCH: Don't *either of you* start up again. Please. Dear God. I'm surprised you don't bicker about what color the bleedin' sky is!

EMMA: Hey! That's… (*realizing*) probably also true.

SASQUATCH: If you ask me, though, you two just need to calm down and stop focusing on what the other one does wrong.

CRAIG: *Again* with the psychoanalysis! Stop trying to tell me what my problems are.

EMMA: Craig's right. You said yourself that you can't come in contact with humans. Meaning you don't have any experience with people.

SASQUATCH: Well, at least you two can agree on something. But do you actually know me well enough to be able to make that judgment? Can you *actually* sit here and tell me, without a shadow of a doubt, that I have no experience with people?

CRAIG: Well, for one thing, you're Bigfoot, so you live alone in the woods like some creepy redneck.

SASQUATCH: Ouch! That's not fair at all. To assume that, because I'm crawling with ticks and I poop in a ditch, I am also an uncultured dolt? That's a horrible generalization, Craig. Do creepy rednecks like cravats? (*he primps his*) Do they have a favorite book? Hmmm? Do they even read? (*melodramatically, mocking him*) Oh, but you're right. There's no depth here. No personality.

CRAIG: I didn't mean–

SASQUATCH: *Great Gatsby*.

EMMA: What?

SASQUATCH: You haven't asked what my favorite book is, so I'm telling you. *Great Gatsby* is my favorite piece of prose. And I'm sure it's simply inconsequential that I enjoy smoking flavored tobacco in the summer and watching the sun set so I can ponder my own existence. Oh, also, I make a fine sorbet, but I can't enter my recipe in any contests because I'm not allowed to leave the woods or come in contact with humans. Not that I would want to because they'd be too busy asking me about the regularity of my bowel movements and how often I mate to try to get to know me. You all think you own this world and you're the only ones who matter. Someday you're all going to find that you're sorely mistaken. But until then, the rest of nature just sits back and takes it. Badgers, deer, squirrels, we all just take it right up the–

CRAIG: We get the picture, thanks.

SASQUATCH: That's right, just shut it off. Ignore it. It proves my point!

EMMA: What? What's your point?

SASQUATCH: My point is you two are so busy bickering with each other, you never stop long enough to realize you're both idiots and hypocrites and whatever else you two call each other. Just like the rest of your species. I call it "*Looney Tune* Syndrome." You laugh at Wile E. Coyote when he fails to catch the Roadrunner, or at Elmer Fudd when Bugs and Daffy beat the snot out of him, but none of you realize the joke is on *you. You* are Elmer. *You* are Wile E.

CRAIG: (*rapt by Sasquatch's monologue*) "*Looney Tunes* Syndrome." Whoa.

SASQUATCH: All amped up with gadgets and conscience and systems, and it still gets you nowhere! And you laugh and think it's funny because of your innate hubris. But it's actually horribly sad, because you keep missing the message: stop overthinking things! Just surrender to the natural flow of things… of life. You've got your heads so far up your own asses, each and every one of you, that you can't see the light of day. You're disconnected from anything that isn't right in front of you. Disassociated, even from your closest companions, so that everyone is just focused on looking better than the next ape. It's aggravating, tiresome, and, frankly, I think I regret helping the two of you. Not that I really had a choice. Not that anything else on *Earth* ever has a choice with you *sapiens*.

Sasquatch stands, brushes his pants off, and walks away.

EMMA: Hey, wait. You can't just leave us here. We had a deal.

SASQUATCH: We did.

EMMA: So, what? You're just gonna ditch us here to think about what we've done?

SASQUATCH: (*shaking his head in disbelief*) There you go assuming again. (*he points*) There's a trail twenty feet to your left that leads back to the park ranger.

Craig and Emma look off in the direction Sasquatch is pointing. He exits without them noticing.

CRAIG: Hey, sorry–

EMMA: We didn't mean to… (*they turn, seeing that he has left*) Oh.

CRAIG: Thank God. I'm gonna explode.

Emma wrinkles her nose, disgusted.

Craig runs off stage gingerly in the direction Sasquatch pointed.

Emma stares back the way they came, processing everything.

EMMA: I'll be right behind you.

Emma considers a moment longer, hesitates, then exits in her own completely different direction.

BLACKOUT

END.

EXECUTIVE DECISIONS III

LIGHTS UP

BEAU, GEORGE, *and* JAX *are all seated around the conference table. Beau taps his pen, reading off the notes in front of him.*

BEAU: Next on the agenda is the racing scene.

JAX: Yes! The pod–chasing stuff! It's great– the setup is great– we loved it, frankly.

BEAU: We did. Yeah.

JAX: But we aren't *in* love with it. Does that make sense?

GEORGE: Um, sure. But, uh... why not?

BEAU: There's concern that fifteen minutes of little pod vehicles zipping around a desert track is going to feel like 'NASCAR in Iraq.' Investors' words, not mine!

GEORGE: Oh, but kids love racing. I see kids at the racetrack all the time.

BEAU: The average attention span for an adult in this country is currently eleven seconds.

JAX: *Seconds*, George. Versus minutes. More minutes than I can count on two hands.

Jax and Beau freeze in position. All the lights dim, save those on George. He looks up, breaking the fourth wall.

GEORGE: (*aside*) At one point in my young life, I deviated from my dream of making a name for myself in racecar circles. I loved the thrill of the chase– watching the road roll away behind me, getting that shot of adrenaline when my fender lined up next to a foe's... man, there was quite a scene for it in California during my younger and more impressionable years... oh, that's good. I should write that down. (*he scribbles a note*) I'm writing about a kid, so I like how that sounded. I'm trying to make Anakin a sympathetic figure, and to do that, I want to see the innocence of his childhood. Uh, Anakin becomes my big bad villain, Darth. Eh, you know. Everyone knows. Except maybe these two idiots. I'm less than amused, but still, I want it! *Need* it! They don't know that. They think I'm just here to get the picture funded. No, I needed notes! Current industry notes from the likes of these peabrains. The same ones who let me keep all my merchandising rights. Short–sighted opportunists. At least their criticism is honest. Everyone else just wants to kiss ass...

GEORGE (*an eerie shift within him*) I have seen other worlds– traveled lightyears in the blink of my mind's eye– and fed it all to you by the shovelful! (*shrugging*) You only live once, I guess... oh, that's good. I should write that down.

George scribbles another note, then turns back to them.

JAX: The investors we have lined up want to keep things current. Three–to–seven–minute scenes, but we're willing to let you drag out some of those laser sword fights if you want.

GEORGE: That feels like it might make the characters a bit... I don't know... two–dimensional, don't you think?

JAX: Please. You've got half a dozen whackadoos with wild–ass names, George. No one's gonna see past the basics. (*in a mocking tone*) "There's the blue sword, the green sword, the princess with antlers and the beeping trashcan with wheels." Nobody's looking for nuance. For instance: you could write every romance scene for this teenager and the nine-year-old in the most stunning poetic verse, and the general public wouldn't know any better. They don't know, they don't care, and they don't care to know. Just give them something flashy and exciting and, in your case, weird– I mean that as a compliment. The point is, just keep writing about frog–ducks in ponds or whatever the hell that first act was about, and don't go overcomplicating things.

BLACKOUT.

FALLING FROM ORBIT

CAST:

MARK – (M) 30s or 40s
ASTRONAUT 1 – (F) about Mark's age
ASTRONAUT 2 – (M) older than Mark
ASTRONAUT 3 – (F or NB) younger than Mark

A NOTE ON PRODUCTION:

The astronauts should function as an ethereal Greek chorus, with synchronized choreography reflecting their anguish. Allow them to haunt the scene. The only essential props/costumes are the dress and the dinosaur mask.

DEBUT PRODUCTION CREDITS:

Produced & performed for Lionface Productions' 2011 Winter One Acts *in Bowling Green, Ohio with the following artists:*

Director: Slade Billew
Mark: Lance Mekeel
Astronaut 1: Trina Friedberg
Astronaut 2: Matthew Gretzinger
Astronaut 3: Meghan Koesters

LIGHTS UP.

A spaceship cockpit. Four sleek control stations sit damaged, flickering alerts and beeping warnings.

ASTRONAUTS 1, 2 & 3 *file in. They wear matching jumpsuits with the word "Casualty" printed boldly across their backs. Their movement is stiff and rigid as they take their seats at the control stations.*

Distorted radio transmissions echo through the cockpit, the voices warped and hauntingly musical. The Astronauts are calm. Their faces are pale, their skin wrinkled and green. In a trance, they stare off at some unseen ethereal force as they speak.

ASTRONAUT 1: I don't remember where we are.

ASTRONAUT 2: I don't know when we left.

ASTRONAUT 3: I don't recall being born…

ASTRONAUT 2: When did we get here?

ASTRONAUT 3: Why did we leave?

ASTRONAUT 1: I don't remember where we came from.

ASTRONAUT 3: Why did we leave?

ASTRONAUT 1: I remember bright lights and shattering glass.

ASTRONAUT 2: I remember teardrops freezing instantly and floating away.

ASTRONAUT 3: I remember rockets sharing their love.

ASTRONAUT 1: It's time to rest.

ASTRONAUT 3: Time to sleep.

ASTRONAUT 2: Time to soar–

ASTRONAUT 1: Through distant stars.

ASTRONAUT 3: I'm cold now.

ASTRONAUT 1: Time is a desert. We are grains of sand.

ASTRONAUT 2: Sand struck by lightning. Turned into glass.

ASTRONAUT 1: Sand can't cling to alien rocks the way moss does.

In unison, the Astronauts turn their heads slowly as MARK *enters. His skin is still pink and healthy, but his breath is ragged. It's a battle for him to stay upright as he crosses to the empty control station.*

ASTRONAUT 1: You're up too late, Mark.

ASTRONAUT 3: Come to bed.

Mark picks up his headset, his hands shaking as he presses a button on his console. If he hears the Astronauts, he does not acknowledge them.

MARK: (*into headset*) Houston, do you copy? (*static hisses*) Where are you, Houston? Do you copy? (*more static*) It all went wrong. It's my fault… I killed them.

The Astronauts lie down like corpses in coffins, a black rose clasped in each of their hands.

MARK: The cockpit's all that's left… I've had a lot of time to think, and I don't regret it. Who's going to remember me? Is anyone out there? Will somebody listen?

ASTRONAUT 1: It's time to sleep, Mark. Time for rest.

MARK: I still hear them. I didn't– none of us knew each other well enough. I wasn't done with them. (*pause*) Christ, that sounds so stupid. It doesn't matter now.

ASTRONAUT 1: Come to bed, Mark.

ASTRONAUT 2: Yes, Mark, come lie down.

ASTRONAUT 3: Do what they say.

ASTRONAUT 1 & 2: Do as we say.

ASTRONAUT 3: Let go, Mark.

MARK: I'm not ready. This isn't right. There's too much here! (*into headset*) Who will remember? When I was a boy, I remember this toy I had. It was a cheap plastic dinosaur. I carried it everywhere. It was my best friend. My father warned me–

During this, Astronaut 3 puts on a dinosaur mask. Astronaut 2 stands slowly and walks up behind Mark.

ASTRONAUT 2: You shouldn't take that into the stadium, Mark. You might lose it. Let's leave it in the car this time. Okay?

MARK: (*like a child*) He wants to come, daddy. It's okay, I'll hold him.

ASTRONAUT 2: It's a busy stadium and there are too many places to drop him where you can't get him back.

MARK: (*like a child*) I want to take him.

ASTRONAUT 2: (*sighing*) All right. But don't say I didn't warn you.

MARK: (*into headset*) You never did discipline me. You got mad and you'd shout, but it was in frustration. You didn't know how to handle me.

ASTRONAUT 2: You never listen, Goddammit!

From this point on, Mark acknowledges the existence of the Astronauts.

MARK: Dad, just calm down. Why are you yelling?

ASTRONAUT 2: Don't talk down to me like that; I'm your father!

MARK: It's not that big a deal! I fixed it!

ASTRONAUT 2: That's not the point– I asked you before not to use these tools without my permission! (*skipping like a scratched record, then–*) How many times do I have to say it?

MARK: I'm sorry. I tried to fix it.

ASTRONAUT 2: (*sighing*) And you did a good job. A fine job, actually. I'm sorry… and I'm proud of your handiwork.

Astronaut 2 sits down. Mark lowers his head, his shoulders drooping.

MARK: I love you too.

ASTRONAUT 3: What about me? You said we were friends!

MARK: I was four.

ASTRONAUT 3: I trusted you. And you dropped me. You left me in a stinking pit of beer and vomit and peanut shells.

MARK: You're not real.

ASTRONAUT 3: You left me.

MARK: We got up to go to the bathroom and I wanted a chili dog. I was hungry and excited, and I had to pee. I left you in my seat and when I came back you were gone. I cried the whole way home.

ASTRONAUT 3: You like making excuses for yourself. Why don't you just listen and understand? People don't want to hear your side of it; they just want to make sure you hurt for them.

Astronaut 3 removes the dinosaur mask and returns to her seat.

ASTRONAUT 1: Things are never as they seem. Let them go. Come to bed, Mark.

MARK: (*into headset*) It's cold out here. But not like ice. Space blankets everything, wraps it in a searing blanket of insignificance, and puts everything in perspective. The cold comes from detachment. From the numbness that persists after your flesh is burnt with passion and truth. It rips you away from everything that matters. The spaceman: he lets it happen. He's driven by exploration but exploring is the problem. It's never done to appreciate. It's always done for profit. I wanted to leave a mark. I wanted the fame, the prestige. I wanted that for myself. *Man* made space cold. He wrote it that way. The only thing cold about space is the hard fact that man has to face his ugly self. Out here, truth burrows under the skin, seeps into your soul, and torments mortality.

ASTRONAUT 2: Sleep will warm you up.

ASTRONAUT 3: No, it will cool you off.

ASTRONAUT 1: It will do both. There is no discomfort when you sleep.

MARK: (*into headset*) I like to imagine that every living soul is like a pane of glass from a beautiful stained–glass window suspended horizontally in space, perpendicular with time. The older we get, the higher our pane rises, and when we die, the pane shatters. If we're lucky, some of our shards are caught by the other panes around us. Eventually, all our leftover shards– the remnants of ourselves we've scattered in this world– they all tumble away into darkness.

ASTRONAUT 2: Your journey is over.

MARK: But my story isn't.

ASTRONAUT 2: Let it go.

MARK: But I'm still here.

ASTRONAUT 1: Not for long.

MARK: Stop it! Just stop. You're useless! Meaningless! All you've done this whole time, every single one of you, is lie here and stink up the oxygen while you rot. This isn't about you.

ASTRONAUT 1 & 2: Come with us.

ASTRONAUT 3: Yes, come.

MARK: I'm not coming with you!

ASTRONAUT 2: We're your friends, Mark. We want what's best for you. You should've come with us when we left, but we came back for you.

ASTRONAUT 1: You won't have another chance.

MARK: I want the ground! I want water and rising tides and leaves that change color. You can't take me back to that. Do you remember? You say we're friends, but do you remember?

ASTRONAUT 1: Memories are for people. You can't have the moon and the stars and hold onto Earth at the same time.

MARK: I can have memories.

ASTRONAUT 2: You shouldn't. They aren't healthy–

ASTRONAUT 3: They'll clog you up, like cholesterol in your arteries.

ASTRONAUT 1: There's nothing left for you here.

MARK: (*collapsing*) I know that! Why do you have to keep saying it?

ASTRONAUT 3: (*after a beat*) There is nothing to fear in death, Mark.

ASTRONAUT: 2: Yes, even the stars die.

ASTRONAUT 3: They burn bright for billions of years and then–

ASTRONAUT 2: One day…

ASTRONAUT 3: *BANG!* They go supernova… like your heart just did today.

Astronaut 3 pokes playfully at Mark's chest.

ASTRONAUT 1: You're barely holding on.

MARK: I'm slipping away…

ASTRONAUT 1: Mark? Mark, sweetie?

Astronaut 1 stands, producing a cocktail dress still on the hanger. She drapes it over herself, leaving the hanger on, and puts her arms through the dress's shoulder straps.

MARK: No. I won't go.

Astronaut 1 steps forward and kneels next to Mark. She grabs him by the hair and yanks his head up. He winces and she strokes his face gently.

ASTRONAUT 1: Mark, sweetie? Are you okay?

MARK: (*fighting tears as his voice involuntarily echoes an old conversation*) Today was just odd. Things were... off.

ASTRONAUT 1: Awe. How so?

MARK: I don't want to talk about it.

ASTRONAUT 1: Fair. How about we go out instead? We've got the whole weekend ahead of us.

MARK: Don't make me.

ASTRONAUT 1: I was hoping you'd say that. Think you could be ready in fifteen?

MARK: Please don't.

Astronaut 1 kisses him on the cheek.

ASTRONAUT 1: I love you.

Astronaut 1 stands and turns away from Mark.

ASTRONAUT 1: (*upset, but unmoving*) I got a call today.

MARK: (*still trembling, shaking his head 'no' as each word escapes. His voice is cold; uncaring.*) Oh?

ASTRONAUT 1: Someone named Vanessa.

MARK: (*his voice is still cold, but horror floods his body*) She… called you?

ASTRONAUT 1: We had a nice long talk.

MARK: Why did she call you?

ASTRONAUT 1: She wanted to apologize.

MARK: What?

ASTRONAUT 1: (*tearing up*) Were you planning on telling me, or were you hoping it would just come out so you wouldn't have to?

MARK: I don't know what to say.

ASTRONAUT 1: Spare me.

MARK: Why would she do that?

ASTRONAUT 1: That's your first thought? What the fuck is wrong with you?

MARK: I was going to say something! It's over, anyway.

ASTRONAUT 1: It's over? It's over! It sure didn't sound like it. You bastard. Seven years. Seven years, Mark! How many times have I asked if something's wrong– If you're okay? It all makes sense now!

MARK: Don't get upse–

Mark clasps his hand over his mouth, muffling the rest of his response. He fights his way over to Astronaut 1. He cradles her head to his chest. She is unresponsive.

MARK: Ella, I'm sorry.

ASTRONAUT 1: How could you?

MARK: I was wrong.

ASTRONAUT 1: Well, you don't have to worry about that.

MARK: You're so beautiful.

ASTRONAUT 1: There's nothing to work through. I'm leaving. You figure things out. I'm not going to make this more painful than it has to be.

MARK: Please stay. Dance with me.

ASTRONAUT 1: Seven years, and this is how you end it. You coward.

MARK: (*crying*) I love you.

Astronaut 3 walks up to Mark and clasps a hand on his shoulder.

ASTRONAUT 3: I wish I knew sooner, man.

MARK: It's fine. I don't want to talk about it.

ASTRONAUT 3: Let's go have a couple beers on me. Just not worry about life for a few hours.

MARK: I've got plans.

ASTRONAUT 3: C'mon, it'll be great. You can pretend you like me, and I'll tell you embarrassing stories you can use to mock me later. It'll be great!

MARK: Stop it, please.

ASTRONAUT 3: That's why we're friends. Remember? I'm a pushover. You can walk all over me. That's what I'm here for. Whatever helps your confidence. I know how much it means to you.

Astronaut 3 puts the dinosaur mask on.

ASTRONAUT 3: (*cont.*) Then you can drop me in the bowels of some concrete coliseum. Your trifling entertainments will be my lonely grave.

Astronaut 2 stands and shoves Mark to the ground. Astronaut 3 kicks him. They circle like jackals, hitting him.

MARK: Please stop!

Blood drips from Mark's mouth. Astronauts 2 & 3 continue to hit him. Mark curls into a ball, unable to fight back. Finally, Astronauts 2 & 3 stop.

MARK: The wand'ring star moves through the night,
Unaware his sinful plight.
He loves too little, lusts too much,
Driven by his wanderlust.
Kill the spaceman's cheery pining,

MARK: (*cont.*) Thrust him from his cradle, whining.
Only in death can life be found,
But spacemen fear life on the ground.
My mind is filled with wondrous journeys,
That suffocate in worldly worries.

ASTRONAUT 1: It's been a bad day; take me dancing.

Mark stands and embraces Astronaut 1. He swings her, initiating a ballroom dance. As Mark sways with Astronaut 1, life gradually slips from her body until she is limp, her feet dragging on the ground as Mark holds her.

Astronauts 2 & 3 lie down.

Mark falls to the floor, collapsing into a heap with Astronaut 1.

MARK: Last night I dreamed I flew from Earth,
To search the stars and find my mirth.
Lightyears later, I touched the ground,
Of purple planet most profound.
The air was rich, the soil too.
The skies were somehow turquoise blue.
The wildlife teemed, plentiful,
Saw me, and all stood sentinel.
So, I asked if I might stay,
And while away my autumn days.
They said I was not welcome there,
Directed me to go elsewhere.
Excused myself, I did to find
Pink sands– a desert in my mind.
I planted seeds, but no palms grew,
Survival seemed for me eschewed.
Next thing I knew, the sands yawned wide,
And swallowed whole my hapless hide.
Those desert sands seeped 'to my soul,

So joys of life might I extol.
Then plasma I melted into,
A yellow star I rippled through.
There, I finally disconnected;
By ego, I was unaffected.
Space isn't space; it's oceans black;
I'm swimming, though the odds are stacked
Against my favor; ship a'wreck'd.
There's nothing more that I respect.
So, softly now to sleep I go,
Without a worry for 'the show.'
It must go on, it will indeed,
But my role it no longer heeds.
That is all well; I'm satisfied,
With how cold space thus ends my ride.
My bed, among the stars I'll make,
I'll rest in peace none may forsake.

The Astronauts sit up sharply.

Mark closes his eyes, his breathing labored.

ASTRONAUT 2: Don't go! We want to stay with you.

ASTRONAUT 1: Can we stay? I don't want to go.

ASTRONAUT 3: Space *is* cold. We were wrong. Come back.

ASTRONAUT 2: We killed him.

ASTRONAUT 1: We could have saved him.

ASTRONAUT 2: We could have saved ourselves.

ASTRONAUT 1: Bring him back! I'm afraid of space.

ASTRONAUT 3: It's lonely here. It's violent and lonely and cold and unkind.

Astronaut 3 sits Mark's corpse upright and leans against it to hold it up. He clenches his eyes shut.

ASTRONAUT 3: I don't want to go. Why did we make him go?

ASTRONAUT 1: He was never with us.

ASTRONAUT 2: My chest hurts. It's fluttering.

Astronaut 2 clenches Mark's corpse.

ASTRONAUT 1: It's too late, now.

Astronaut 1 lies down in front of Mark, clinging to his legs. The Astronauts close their eyes.

The cockpit glows with ethereal light. The radio hisses, playing eerie distorted music that carries the scene away.

BLACKOUT

END.

EXECUTIVE DECISIONS IV

LIGHTS UP

BEAU, GEORGE *and* JAX *are all seated around the conference table.*

George's face is scrunched up; he's strongly considering something.

JAX: Hey, George? You still with us?

GEORGE: Your notes are making me ponder now…

JAX: Good! Care to ponder aloud?

BEAU: Maybe we can be of help?

GEORGE: Well, it's just… all these notes you have on *Phantom*, they're hitting on some insecurities and reservations I have with the project. Part of me wonders what would happen if I just called back Harry, Carrie, and Mark. Are either of you familiar with Mara Jade? From the fiction books based on my movies?

JAX: (*chuckling*) My interns read for me these days, George. It's not something I find 'fun.'

BEAU: I'm more of a *National Geographic* kind of reader.

GEORGE: Okay, so no. Well, she's a brilliant character. The author who invented her did an outstanding job– I hate his guts! Anyway, It's all still mine, right? And I thought, we've got this character already, and she's practically written for me, but what if she goes to the Dark Side somehow? And that's Luke's next salvation mission? Instead of saving his dad, he's trying to save the woman he loves, and she's just completely succumbed to the power of the Dark Side. The Force is what gets between them and their relationship, and, of course, Luke won't want to split up his family. They have a son, Ben, who is also Force-sensitive.

JAX: We could rebrand a whole new trilogy! Star *Divorce.* Really complex, George. I'm with you so far.

BEAU: Really?

JAX: Who can't relate to that?

BEAU: Your target demo, for one. Eight- to twelve-year-old boys aren't going to relate to a divorce story.

JAX: Kids watch their parents go through divorce! That's what I keep thinking these past few months. I keep saying, "Thank God I don't have kids, or Lydia would make this an even bigger mess." I slept in the doghouse one night. In the *actual* dog's house out back. I mean, I tried to sleep in the car, but she locked me out and my keys were still in the house!

BEAU: (*aside to George, overlapping the above*) His wife left him about four months ago. Very sensitive subject.

GEORGE: (*to them both*) That's pretty rough.

JAX: Keep going, George. I like your idea. I think you've got something.

GEORGE: Well, as you know, once the movies were over, Luke went on to re-establish a temple for young padawans. With Leia as part of the New Republic, Luke also has access to people in all the highest places across the galaxy. So, I thought, if he's wrapped up trying to save his wife from the Dark Side, what if she tries to seduce him with his own grasp of power? Because she's loving the things she can do with her powers as a baddie. And Luke keeps going between good and evil, right and wrong. She essentially turns him. She wants the two of them to kill off the Senate and establish their own Empire, with Force-sensitive beings at the top of the new social order. It corrupts everything Luke loves about the Force, but it keeps his relationship pure and intact, and he falls.

JAX: You could even call one of 'em 'The Fall of Skywalker,' or something.

GEORGE: Ooooh, I should write that down!

JAX: See, George, this is what we're talking about! This is the George we were hoping to see. This is-

BEAU: (*reviewing his notes*) It's the Scottish play.

JAX: What?

GEORGE: Huh?

BEAU: Apart from the names, I mean. The formula for this is just the Scottish play.

JAX: You keep saying that like we're supposed to know what it means. What the hell is the Scottish play?

BEAU: It's Shakespeare.

GEORGE: I've definitely never heard of a play called *The Scottish Play* by Shakespeare.

JAX: Yeah, that sounds nothing like a Shakespeare title.

BEAU: It's not the actual name, it's a nickname because you aren't supposed to say the actual title: it's cursed!

GEORGE: Oh, *Macbeth*? Are you talking about *Macbeth*?

BEAU: You're not supposed to say the word!

GEORGE: That's only if you're in a theater! (*the actor may pause to regard the audience before continuing*) And even still, if you are, you can say it if you're in a production of *Macbeth*.

JAX: I hope you're sure because otherwise you just cursed the whole damn office building.

BEAU: Either way, your plot is *Macbeth* and critics are smart enough to see through that.

GEORGE: (*proudly*) I've never read *Macbeth.*

BEAU: Then how do you know so much about it?

GEORGE: (*shrugging*) How do *you*? I thought you said you didn't read anything but *National Geographic.*

BEAU: Film adaptations, obviously.

GEORGE: Oh.

BEAU: The plot device is far too recognizable, George. The wife of a royal is corrupted by power and convinces him they should kill everyone and take over. And you do *not* want to let a critic catch you lifting ideas from any of Shakespeare's best-known works. It's as elementary as three Billie goats about to cross a troll's bridge.

JAX: Shit. He's right, George. I'm sorry.

George tucks those notes back in his bag, shrinking somewhat into his chair as he does.

BLACKOUT.

UNDER THE BRIDGE

CAST:

FILTH – (M, F or NB) under 30.
MADDIE – (F) age 18–24.
RANKENFILCH – (M) age 40+. A foul bridge troll.

ORIGINAL PRODUCTION CREDITS:

Produced & performed for Lionface Productions' 2012 Winter One Acts *in Bowling Green, Ohio with the following artists:*

Director: Andrea Miller
Corpse (*now* Filth): Colton Watkins
Maddie: Brittany Pausch
Haufronken (*now* Rankenfilch): Scott Stechschulte

LIGHTS UP.

A wooden bridge stretches over a narrow surging stream in the depths of a dense forest. Beneath the bridge rests a cave. Next to the cave, the embers of a dying campfire crackle.

Opposite the fire, FILTH, *an emaciated young person, lies crumpled in a pile of dead leaves. He is shackled to the bridge, chewing on his fingernails, jittery and nervous as a rodent. Where his left leg should be, there is only a bloody stump.*

MADDIE, *an angelic teenager in medieval robes, enters, gliding along the forest trail. She hesitates as the bridge creaks and groans. Filth notices her.*

FILTH: Go away!

MADDIE: Oh, gosh! What on Earth–?

FILTH: Hurry, get out!

MADDIE: Are you alright?

FILTH: Leave. Leave this place! Get away.

MADDIE: You're hurt. Here, I'll help. I always carry antiseptic in case I get a scratch.

FILTH: No, stay back. Go back where you came from.

MADDIE: I can't do that. I have to get to the village across the bridge.

FILTH: You'll never get across.

MADDIE: Oh, yes. Never mind that. You're chained. Why are you chained?

FILTH: What?

MADDIE: You've been chained up.

FILTH: Oh, that. That is just... that is how it is. I, uh... I am Filth. Yes, I am filth. And filth– it must be held down. Suppressed. That is the way of things.

MADDIE: That's funny talk. You're funny. I like you.

FILTH: No. There is nothing to like here.

Maddie digs through her purse, producing a tube of liquid band-aid. She unscrews the cap, squirting a large glob of day-glow bright ointment on her index finger.

MADDIE: Here. Ointment. Let me see your hand.

FILTH: What... um... what do I do?

MADDIE: Take it off my finger and rub it on your, uh...

Filth scoops the ointment off her finger.

FILTH: Where?

MADDIE: Well... on your... stump. On your stump, there, I guess. Your leg.

Filth smears the ointment on his bloody stump. He shudders, grasping at it and rocking back and forth.

FILTH: Ow! It burns! Burns!

MADDIE: It's okay. Don't worry. It'll go away in a minute.

FILTH: Ssshhh! Quiet! Must be quiet.

MADDIE: But you're the one making all the noise.

FILTH: He'll hear. Ssshhh!

A roar echoes through the cave. Filth squirms, fighting pain from the antiseptic on his open wounds.

RANKENFILCH *the troll enters, crawling out of the cave, his hands clutched around his bulbous, wart–covered stomach. He is a grotesque creature matted with patches of wiry hair.*

RANKENFILCH: Shut up! Stop that infernal ruckus, you decrepit little filth!

FILTH: Sorry. Sorry– I'm sorry.

RANKENFILCH: Eat your foot.

FILTH: I have antiseptic on–

RANKENFILCH: Eat. Your. Foot!

Filth tears small pieces of meat from his leg and eats them. This action must occur, it should not simply be mimed.

MADDIE: Oh, no. Don't make him do that!

RANKENFILCH: What? Who the hell are you? Giving me orders... are you from the queen? So, what if you are? If she wants to micromanage me, she best come down here and give the orders herself!

MADDIE: I will take no such message to Her Majesty.

FILTH: She's a traveler.

RANKENFILCH: Shut your trap!

FILTH: She is.

RANKENFILCH: I heard you the first time.

MADDIE: My name's Maddie.

RANKENFILCH: Maddie the traveler.

MADDIE: Just Maddie.

RANKENFILCH: But you are traveling?

MADDIE: Yes, well, I– yes.

RANKENFILCH: Which means you want to cross the bridge, eh?

MADDIE: Well, I'm in no real hurry. But yes. I have to cross the bridge to get where I'm going.

RANKENFILCH: And where might that be?

MADDIE: Brambleton.

RANKENFILCH: Why?

MADDIE: Does it matter?

RANKENFILCH: Of course, it bloody well matters! Accursed girl. I control the traffic of feet… and goods… what goes across my bridge. Otherwise, all kinds of Rexport contraband would end up out in the hills, with the lesser folk.

MADDIE: (*a resigned sigh*) In that case, I am off to visit relatives in Brambleton and Bluffsburg… and, as such, I shall try not to take offense to your suggestion that my cousins are 'lesser folk.'

RANKENFILCH: If you *do* take offense, let me know. There's an extra crossing fee for taking anything over this fine bridge.

MADDIE: Wha–?

RANKENFILCH: Now, open your satchel. Let's have a look.

Rankenfilch swipes Maddie's bag from her. She swats at him, knocking the leather satchel from his hands. A dozen nude drawings of people and mythical beasts flutter forth from the falling satchel.

Rankenfilch picks up a drawing, squints, then adjusts. It unfurls like a centerfold.

The troll peers first at the blank back, holding the extra-large nude sketch up towards the audience. Then, he turns the drawing over and recoils, dropping it and gagging.

RANKENFILCH: In the name of goodness, what fresh smut is this? You horrible little trollop! You're smuggling sins into the queen's provincial towns!

MADDIE: I never!

During this exchange, Maddie scrambles to collect her drawings. Rankenfilch snatches most of them up first.

RANKENFILCH: What else do you sell, you wench?

MADDIE: They're just my drawings, you wretched old pustule!

Rankenfilch gestures for Maddie to hand over the stack of drawings she picked up. Reluctantly, she obliges.

Rankenfilch shuffles all the drawings into a neat stack as he explains.

RANKENFILCH: This is exactly why my checkpoint exists! The whole kingdom would implode with lust if I weren't here to stop the spread of smut pamphlets… and *whoring.*

MADDIE: How dare you!

RANKENFILCH: It's not a far cry from porn peddling; I can tell you that!

MADDIE: These drawings are none of your business, and my possession of them does not make me a whore. I'm an artist. Now, let me pass!

RANKENFILCH: You may not.

MADDIE: I was told I don't actually need your permission.

RANKENFILCH: To cross *my* bridge, you do!

MADDIE: The bridge is a bridge. It exists to be crossed.

RANKENFILCH: Then why ask my permission in the first place?

MADDIE: Because– because your home is under there. I wanted to be polite. I know about you. Everyone knows. You're despicable. And miserable. And manipulative–

RANKENFILCH: And rank and foul-breathed and disgusting… and I'm a judgmental old generalizer, to boot! Yes… and I'm in charge of this bridge.

MADDIE: Do you own the bridge?

FILTH: The queen owns the bridge.

Rankenfilch backhands Filth, who shrieks.

RANKENFILCH: Shut up, you!

FILTH: Just the facts. Just the truth. Nothing filthy.

RANKENFILCH: Save that it passed through your filthy lips.

FILTH: (*defeated*) Oh.

MADDIE: Don't be so cruel.

RANKENFILCH: He must learn discipline. He's my filthy pet. Mine to raise. To discipline.

MADDIE: What you're doing isn't discipline. It's torture.

RANKENFILCH: Who are you to tell me? Just another pissant human throwing your weight around.

MADDIE: Well, at least I'm not claiming ownership of a bridge that rightfully belongs to Her Highness.

RANKENFILCH: That bridge is my bridge. I get paid to let the community use it.

MADDIE: I don't see your name on it anywhere.

Rankenfilch points to a post on the bridge where the words 'Rankenfilch's Bridge*' have been hastily gouged into the wood.*

RANKENFILCH: (*under his breath*) I told her majesty I needed a bigger sign. (*louder*) There, right there. It says 'Rankenfilch's Bridge.' That's my name. On the bridge. It's mine. See the apostrophe–S? That gives my name possession. And what does it refer to? The bridge! Ergo, it is *my* bridge.

MADDIE: Right. You'll excuse me if I don't subscribe to school lessons from a bitter old chode.

She turns and climbs up to the bridge. Rankenfilch dives, grabbing her by the arm, and throws her to the ground.

RANKENFILCH: I said no!

MADDIE: Don't you dare touch me! Get off!

RANKENFILCH: As if you would be sullied by my touch.

MADDIE: Get off now, you putrid old ass-belch! Or I'll tell the queen!

Rankenfilch stops, backing away, and Maddie scrambles to her feet.

RANKENFILCH: You wouldn't tell her. No. (*shaking his head*) So what if you did? What do I care?

MADDIE: If I did, you'd be hanged.

RANKENFILCH: No. I'm just doing my job. She wouldn't! It's my bridge. And I can't just let anyone over the bridge. Especially debauchery–peddling whores.

MADDIE: Enough! I will tolerate many, many things in order to keep cordial, but I will *not* stand for your crass and presumptuous accusations of scandal! (*a beat*) You know, everyone is afraid to come in here and cross your bridge because you're such a miserable stump of a man–

RANKENFILCH: Troll!

MADDIE: Troll. Fine… sorry. (*beat*) Everyone told me, "Go around the wood. It takes longer but you'll avoid that rotten troll."

RANKENFILCH: I know what they all think. I don't care! Life is wretched. People are wretched. No one else seems to notice. You all worry about going to hell when you die– ha! Hell is here because of the lot of you!

Rankenfilch points to a wooden sign with the phrase 'Hell is here' *finger–painted in dung and caked with fungi.*

MADDIE: I think you've just lost sight of what's important in life. Or maybe you lost what was important to you. But you're an ignorant fool if you think that entitles you to act like this– to be like this.

RANKENFILCH: You stupid brat! What do you know about life? You're barely old enough to wipe your own arsehole! You haven't been around long enough to know how anything works. Except that there's money in sex. Ha! Yes, you've certainly figured out the meaning of life: life without care or responsibility. Maybe I should purchase a floral bustier to perk up my titties and commission you to draw a raunchy nude of me. I'll go get a nice close shave so my thighs squeak when I walk. (*in falsetto*) "Here's a naked drawing of me– that should be enough to cover room and board for a fortnight, right?" (*scoffing*) If only life were so easy!

MADDIE: What is wrong with you, you cruel, sad creature? Nothing will change your mind, I see, regardless the topic… you're going to die alone.

RANKENFILCH: If only I could be so lucky! I want to die alone. You know, the Greek philosophers had it right. Life is shit and people are the maggots who crawl all over it, eating all they can.

MADDIE: I don't think a philosopher ever said that.

RANKENFILCH: People are evil and stupid! No one is good by nature.

MADDIE: (*pointing to Filth*) What about him? What was his great and terrible sin?

RANKENFILCH: This filth? He crossed the bridge with dirty boots. Tracked cow shit or deer shit or some kind of shit all over the structure. The planks, the ropes holding the plank– it was despicable.

FILTH: But I already told you I didn't know there was poo on my boots!

RANKENFILCH: (*roaring with rage*) You are filth, maggot! You are unfit for society when feces follow you like ducklings. Now sit down, shut up, and eat your dirty foot!

MADDIE: You're punishing him for an honest mistake?

RANKENFILCH: (*laughing derisively*) If you believe *his* story.

MADDIE: I think I've pieced together the *whole* story, actually.

RANKENFILCH: The whole story according to who? To you? This isn't your job, and this isn't your bridge! It's *mine* and it's *mine*, and *I* say Filth here (*pointing to Filth*) can't be trusted. Trust no one, that's the key. Like you. I knew I couldn't trust you as soon as I saw you. The minute your satchel flies open, out pops the pornography.

MADDIE: It's not–

RANKENFILCH: Not pornography. Sure, sure. Except that it *is* pornography, and if I let it cross my bridge, they'll hold me liable for trafficking indecencies or some damn thing! You tempestuous little titmouse!

MADDIE: Is anything beautiful in your eyes, I wonder?

RANKENFILCH: Oh, please! Your vanity is bewildering. I've seen prettier girls than you.

MADDIE: I wasn't talking about me! My God, you think you've got it all figured out. Fine. You sit here in your little bog of bitterness. But don't take it out on everyone else!

Maddie pulls a pair of bolt cutters from her purse. She crosses to Filth, who watches her with eyes as big as a puppy's.

Rankenfilch raises an eyebrow. As she extends the cutters to Filth's shackles, she glares.

RANKENFILCH: Don't you dare.

Rankenfilch picks up a rock, ready to swing.

Defiantly, Maddie snips Filth's shackles.

MADDIE: Go ahead. You're free!

Filth sniffles, struggling to stand up.

MADDIE: Go on. I've freed you. Cross the bridge. Hurry!

FILTH: I can't. I've only got one leg. I can't run anymore.

RANKENFILCH: Unbelievable! Where the hell do you think he's going? No place in a hurry, that's for sure!

Filth wriggles away from the camp.

Rankenfilch cackles, his belly shaking.

MADDIE: It doesn't matter where he goes. Or if he goes. So long as he has the option to go! You can't keep him here against his will, especially for such a silly mistake. And as for me, I'm crossing the bridge. I have the queen's permission to cross through here and that's all I need. My conscience is clear.

RANKENFILCH: Fine! Go ahead. But I'm watching you. If I see so much as a finger drawn without garments, I'll know you drew it, and I'll report it to her majesty straightaway!

MADDIE: Be my guest. Her majesty is well aware of my artistic endeavors. She's commissioned me to do the illustrations for a royal book of science on the creatures of the kingdom. (*she produces a paper with several wax seals on it*) This is my royal decree to pass through these parts as I want.

RANKENFILCH: Why didn't you say so?

MADDIE: Because Her Majesty still empathizes with you, for some unholy reason, even though half the kingdom wants you fired. She insists you aren't as bad as the stories. She asked me to go this way and see what you'd do.

RANKENFILCH: A test?

MADDIE: An investigation into your misconduct.

RANKENFILCH: Misconduct? Misconduct!

MADDIE: Yes! And boy, did you fail!

Maddie produces another scroll with seals on it, presenting it to Rankenfilch.

RANKENFILCH: What? No!

MADDIE: For which, you will be hanged. (*leaning in, enjoying his panic*) You're going to die alone. You say you don't care, but I don't think that's true… You're also going to die here, which I'm sure you *claim* you'd prefer, but deep down, you wish you'd seen more of the world. Had some kind of journey. Learned something about yourself. And I think it eats away at you. (*she locks eyes with him*) Have a nice day.

Maddie skips assuredly across the bridge.

Rankenfilch opens his mouth to protest, but stops, scratching his head. He glares at her, his face turning pink. Then, he lobs the rock at his home. It collapses in on itself.

With a growl, Rankenfilch slumps down into a pile of dead leaves.

BLACKOUT

END.

EXECUTIVE DECISIONS V

LIGHTS UP

BEAU *stands, leaning over awkwardly to show* JAX *his notes.* GEORGE *still sits across from them, waiting patiently.*

BEAU: So, um... next note here, Jax. We have... uh... Skid Fist–

GEORGE: Kit Fisto! Oh, he's one of my favorites.

JAX: We can't do it.

GEORGE: (*forlorn*) But why?!

JAX: 'Kid–fister,' George! It sounds like 'kid fister.' Can you really not hear that? Because I can, and that's how I read the damn thing, and it's just not gonna fly! Okay? And don't get me started on the focus groups. I mean, I gotta sell this to kids, George! Christ.

BEAU: He never says that.

JAX: My mother would plotz if she heard me say that.

Jax pushes back from the table, burying his face in his hands. He sits there a moment, then rubs his temples.

GEORGE: Oh, give Kit a chance, Jax. I think kids will love him, really, He's an underwater Jedi–

BEAU: (*to self*) So that's how you say that–

GEORGE: He's an amphibian, so he breathes underwater and uses his laser sword underwater.

BEAU: (*still to self*) I thought it was a soft 'J,' like 'yeti.'

GEORGE: His hair is actually tentacles…. and he's green. Kids love green! Kermit the Frog, Oscar the Grouch... Yoda! I mean, Kit's a real winner. Gonna sell a lot of action figures... a lot.

JAX: (*muttering*) That only helps you, George.

BEAU: What if you simply renamed him?

GEORGE: I'd have to have Lucas Arts reprogram three video games! I'd have to contact Kenner about the action figure! There's a Jedi Temple sleeping bag he was supposed to be on…

JAX: Hold on. George, are you developing merchandise *before* you've found producers for your film?

GEORGE: More like simultaneously.

BEAU: Surely that merch hasn't been printed yet, though. The character's image wouldn't change, just his name.

JAX: Beau's right, George! After all, what's in a name?

GEORGE: Don't get Freudian with me!

Beau shakes his head, his shoulders drooping notably.

GEORGE: 'What's in a name?' Ha! *Everything.* Do you know how long I played with letter combinations to get a name I liked? I spend hours charting these things out, and *months* imagining them as I paint a picture of who they are. That's what goes into a name! You can't just take my name and flip it upside-down. What if I was referencing a beloved film professor or… or a deceased child!

JAX: (*accusatory*) You don't have any dead kids!

GEORGE: You don't know that! This is Hollywood, for fuck's sake! Oh, crackers, now you've got me cursing, too. I really am having a breakdown. Look at me… am I sweating? I feel cold. Oh, God! It could be another panic attack. Oh god, oh god, oh god!

George curls up in a ball on the floor, perhaps hiding under the table.

BEAU: George?

JAX: George! Hey? (*aside*) Whoa! I gave George a panic attack. (*fanning himself*) They're gonna fuckin' fire me for this! If word gets out, I'll be the laughingstock of town. Shit! Shit, shit, shit!

Jax ducks into the corner and snorts a line of coke.

BEAU: Jax?

George rocks on the floor, where he repeats his mantra:

GEORGE: Kit Fisto. Kit Fisto. Kit Fisto…

BEAU: (*a beat*) Okay, everyone, let's reel it in. I think renaming Kit isn't the best idea. Maybe we just keep him in the background, and you can do a cartoon or something later.

GEORGE: Oh, that's great. The tentacles are gonna really sell, I'm tellin' ya'. Studies show kids love tentacles!

Seemingly recovered, Jax stands back up quickly, cocking his head.

Jax: Why? Because of those Japanese cartoons?

Beau buries his face in his hands.

BLACKOUT.

CALL ME JERRY

CAST:

NORMAN – (M) 55–70. An old grouch with no time for nonsense. Perhaps the least whimsical, rail-thin bloke in existence…

JERRY – (M, F, or NB) Any age. Hoarse and loud and blissfully unaware of the universe. Somewhat mad from millennia alone, Jerry is an overly animated creature of comfort…

ORIGINAL PRODUCTION CREDITS:

Produced & performed for Theta Alpha Phi's Fall 2008 Shortsfest *in Bowling Green, Ohio with the following artists:*

Director: Brent Winzek
Larry (*now* Jerry): Casey Tony
Norman: Zachary Navarre

A NOTE ON PRODUCTION:

The interdimensional jacuzzi can be represented by anything as simple as rehearsal blocks and chairs. A fog machine and low, saturated lighting should help set an ethereal mood.

In darkness, the sound of bubbles crescendos.

LIGHTS UP.

A jet–black jacuzzi, shrouded in darkness and fog. Blue and orange lights pulsate from unseen celestial bodies as NORMAN*'s corpse sits lifeless against the outside of the jacuzzi, his neck crooked, his jaw slack. A cigarette hangs limply from the old man's mouth and his sunglasses are cockeyed on his face. His tank top and Hawaiian swim trunks are foul and grease stained.*

JERRY, *a jolly humanoid fish creature, rises from the hot tub's waters. His face has intricate black, white, and orange markings, like a clown fish, and his hair looks solid and shiny, a vibrant tuft of electric orange tangled in a mass atop his head, adorned, perhaps, with starfish and seashells.*

Jerry looks around nervously, checking to make sure the coast is clear, then he spits a stream of water onto Norman's face.

JERRY: (*his voice deep and hoarse, but jolly*) Wake up, creature! Behold my heated water container!

Norman's corpse does not move. Jerry leans daintily over the side of the jacuzzi and pokes at Norman.

NORMAN: (*coming to*) Uh, oh, sorry– what?

JERRY: Wake up. You've arrived at my tub of heat!

NORMAN: Huh? Who the hell are you?

JERRY: (*imitating a dramatic echo*) I am the guardian of this heated water container and you... you have released me from the duties I've been charged with.

NORMAN: Okay.

Norman shivers, his breath ragged. He rubs his arms, trying to warm himself.

JERRY: Are you cold?

NORMAN: It's freezing!

JERRY: That's why the water's warm, friend. (*patting the surface of the water*) C'mon in.

NORMAN: No, thanks... What happened to me?

JERRY: You drowned.

NORMAN: Drowned?

JERRY: You're dead.

NORMAN: I don't understand.

JERRY: You're feeling *deathly* cold because you're *deathly* dead!

NORMAN: Dead? I'm dead?!

JERRY: Drowned. You drowned! You got water in your lungs, and you died. You're dead.

NORMAN: But I don't remember it.

JERRY: Well, you're here, and you're cold, so you must be dead. That's the only way to get here.

Norman stands, still shivering, but bold in his actions. He nods to himself as he hops up on the edge of the jacuzzi and swings his feet over the side.

NORMAN: Ah, I see. I think I follow you.

JERRY: You do?

NORMAN: Yeah. This is clearly a dream. I left the window open again or something. Now move over, it's freezing.

JERRY: It gets cold. That's why the water's warm, friend.

NORMAN: No, the water's warm because my mind is offering solutions. I left the window open, and now my brain is conjuring hot tubs. (*to himself*) Or it's that medication. Christ, this is trippy.

Norman eases into the water, sighing with relief. Jerry is visibly excited about this.

JERRY: (*suppressing giddy glee*) So...

NORMAN: So... you say I'm dead?

JERRY: Uh huh. That's the only way to get here, like I said. So, you must be dead! I'm free! You're stuck!

NORMAN: I'm stuck! Where am I stuck?

JERRY: (*playfully*) What's your name?

NORMAN: My name's Norman.

JERRY: Can I call you Norm?

NORMAN: What?

JERRY: It's short for Norman... you know... 'Norm' without the 'An.'

NORMAN: Yeah, yeah. I get it.

JERRY: So, I can call you Norm?

NORMAN: Only if I can call you fish, or gills, or–

JERRY: Jerry.

NORMAN: What?

JERRY: Call me Jerry. All my friends call me Jerry.

NORMAN: Oh, so that's your name.

JERRY: No.

NORMAN: So why–

JERRY: Jerry.

NORMAN: But just–

JERRY: Jerry!

NORMAN: If you–

JERRY: *JEH–REE!*

NORMAN: Okay! *Jerry*... why are you here?

JERRY: (*imitating a dramatic echo again*) To make sure– sure– sure– sure– sure!

NORMAN: To make sure of what?

JERRY: Uh, y'know... To make sure– sure– sure– sure– sure.

NORMAN: But that doesn't make sense! Are you making sure the hot tub's not attacked? Or does it have magical powers you need to keep from falling into the wrong hands? What're you making sure of?

JERRY: Uh... I, uh... I was never told.

NORMAN: How long have you been here?

Like a bashful child, Jerry avoids eye contact and mumbles something unintelligibly.

NORMAN: What was that?

JERRY: Just under a millennium...

NORMAN: Uh huh. And what have you been doing here?

JERRY: Y'know... Stuff!

NORMAN: Great.

They sit in awkward silence.

Norman crosses his arms and looks off in the distance. Jerry watches him quietly, fighting the urge to keep talking.

They make eye contact for a moment and Jerry opens his mouth to speak, but Norman rolls his eyes and shakes his head, looking away again.

JERRY: So, Norm... what's your dimension like?

NORMAN: My dimension?

JERRY: Yeah. This heated water container is on its own plane of existence. No one is from here.

NORMAN: Where is here? Y'know what? Fuck it. I won't even remember this when I wake up.

JERRY: But you won't wake up... unless you fall asleep... but I've never fallen asleep here.

NORMAN: C'mon, just splash some water on me or something so I wake up.

JERRY: No! You might drown... again!

Awkward silence ensues. Norman tries to stand, but an unseen force tugs him back in.

NORMAN: Don't touch me! Let me go!

JERRY: I'm not keeping you here!

NORMAN: Then why can't I get out?

JERRY: Because you got in!

NORMAN: You told me to get in!

JERRY: Why did you listen to me? No one ever listens to me.

NORMAN: Well, you didn't say that! You just said, 'The water's warm, friend. C'mon in!'

JERRY: I didn't think you would!

NORMAN: Obviously I got in! It's freezing.

Awkward silence ensues again.

JERRY: You don't think you're dead, do you?

NORMAN: I am sitting in an interdimensional jacuzzi with a fish–man who isn't named Jerry but likes it when people call him Jerry: of course I'm not dead! I probably just took too many liver pills. I have a liver condition, Jerry. I also cheated on my wife *twice*. And it doesn't matter that I'm telling you this because I'll wake up any minute!

JERRY: You drowned.

NORMAN: Yeah, sure. I caught that part.

JERRY: You're stuck here, Norm.

NORMAN: You mentioned. Care to enlighten me?

JERRY: No... you'll be mad.

NORMAN: No, I won't because none of this is real. Go ahead, take your best shot.

JERRY: Well... the hot tub you died in exists in the same place in at least twelve different dimensions. When you died, the space-time filtration system sucked your soul into this dimension before it could get away… allegedly, this is due to a recall on the faulty positron collider.

NORMAN: Easy. Just call customer service and get a repairman out here. If they have hot tubs, they're bound to have hot tub repairmen.

JERRY: I tried… twice. Once, after the first two years, and then again, three years later.

NORMAN: And?

JERRY: The first time, the replacement part was on backorder. They put me on the waiting list, but they never called back. I got the same automated system, I plugged in my case number, and it would say 'processing: parts on backorder.' Then, someone finally showed up after three more years had passed. They apologized for the inconvenience, explained that the company had filed Chapter Eleven– I don't like books, so I'm not sure I get the reference– and, uh… oh, yeah, they filed Chapter Eleven and would no longer be manufacturing the parts to repair my hot tub. They refunded me on a Visa cash card. (*he pulls the card from his armpit or hair*). I explained to them that I was soul-bonded to the filter, and I needed them to cut me loose, but there wasn't anything they could do! They left me here!

Jerry breaks down in tears.

NORMAN: Bullshit. I'll wake up any minute.

JERRY: (*his sadness evaporates in a blink*) You're stuck here now. You have to make sure– sure– sure– sure.

NORMAN: Wait, wait, wait. You said you had to make sure.

JERRY: I did.

NORMAN: So, you have to make sure.

JERRY: No, I *had* to make sure. You got in the water, so you take my spot.

NORMAN: Absolutely not!

JERRY: Absolutely yes, Norm.

NORMAN: Stop calling me Norm!

JERRY: Can I call you Jerry?

NORMAN: NO!

JERRY: Don't get upset. I did that and it took twice as long for you to show up.

NORMAN: (*taking a deep breath*) Well, Jerry, what do I have to do here until I wake up?

JERRY: You drowned.

NORMAN: You've already said that!

JERRY: (*singing*) Temper.

NORMAN:(*collecting himself*) Jerry?

JERRY: Yes?

NORMAN: Could you please answer me: what do I have to make sure of?

JERRY: Not sure, Norm. I never did figure that out. Thanks to you, I don't have to!

Jerry pulls a suitcase and a fedora from the hot tub, shakes off some water, and exits right.

Norman sits silently for a moment before trying to pull himself out of the jacuzzi. He struggles, straining against some unseen force, but cannot get himself out of the hot tub.

NORMAN: Son of a bitch.

BLACKOUT

END.

EXECUTIVE DECISIONS VI

LIGHTS UP

GEORGE *makes notes on his screenplay pages.*

JAX *stands, hands crossed behind his back as he stares out a large 'window.'*

BEAU *drums his pencil on the table, regarding George.*

BEAU: (*sighing*) You really had something with those first three, George, but... we just aren't sure...

JAX: (*without turning around*) We're not sure you've got it anymore, old man. This script has a lot of problems. The dialogue, for instance– it's so damn whiny!

GEORGE: You said you don't have any kids, is that right?

JAX: That's right.

GEORGE: Take my advice: you wanna know about kids? Go to the action figure section of any retail store, and just wait and listen. It won't take long for you to realize all kids *do* is whine. They're just like critics! Hell, they may even be worse! (*he smacks his script*) They'll totally relate.

BEAU: That's… a fair point, actually.

JAX: Maybe another motion picture isn't the right answer. The script feels so rushed, and clearly you have more ideas than you know what to do with. Have you considered some kind of TV series?

GEORGE: Okay. All right. Now, we're on the same wavelength. I hear you on this. I think I have exactly what you're looking for. Great for kids– music, fun, mayhem. It's about a group of interstellar jazz artists– think *Scooby-Doo* but with a band.

George stands up straight. He clicks a projector on, revealing concept art for The Jizz Wailers.[1]

JAX: '*Jizz* Wailers,' George– seriously? Is this a joke to you? Fuck off with this nonsense!

Jax and Beau storm out, shaking their heads.

George shrugs, collecting his things. Poignantly, he stops, turns to the audience, and adjusts his glasses.

GEORGE: Everyone's a critic these days…

BLACKOUT

END.

---

[1] Yes, that's actual canon. Look it up if you don't believe us but watch those safe search settings…

This marks the end of the script for a complete production of *Alas, Poor Uranus.*

EXECUTIVE DECISIONS

Continuous Script

CAST:

GEORGE – (M) 60s, overweight with white hair & beard.

BEAU BASIC – (M or F) 50s, uptight but smart producer in their own head.

JAX WEISSMAN – (M) 30s or 40s, cut-throat, fast-talking producer.

PRODUCTION NOTES:

This is the continuous version of the script for the one-act *Executive Decisions.*

LIGHTS UP

A mid-1990s corporate Hollywood conference room sits empty apart from GEORGE, *who wears a plaid flannel shirt tucked into his jeans. He sits at the end of the conference table, shuffling script pages, peering at them through tiny glasses perched at the end of his nose.*

He puts the pages down and pulls out two miniature spaceships, holding them up at different angles as if his eye were a camera lens.

JAX WEISSMAN *and* BEAU BASIC *burst through the conference room's double doors, or fly in from the rafters, landing on the table like it's a helipad.*

JAX: Sorry we're late, George. Completely my fault. Well, between us three, I blame the bitch I've got on my latest project.

GEORGE: Oh. (*shaking his head*) I'm sorry, please don't use that term.

JAX: Are you– ? (*turning to Beau*) Is he serious? (*back to George*) Are you fuckin' serious?

GEORGE: I–

JAX: Remind me, was it your movie that gave Carrie an eating disorder? Y'know, because you insisted on putting her in a metal bikini for nearly five minutes of screen time.

GEORGE: It's un–

JAX: Did you know that Beau here got his start producing pornos, eh? Did you know that?

GEORGE: No, but–

JAX: How long's your average porn, Beau?

BEAU: Anywhere from ten minutes to two hours. But we find that most men usually focus on no more than three minutes of screen time.

JAX: (*nodding triumphantly*) Bang. That's what I was looking for. Thank you, Beau. (*to George*) Ya' hear that, Grandpa Feminism? You made that poor girl wear that thing for more screen time than your average crank–yanker.

GEORGE: (*defeated*) No one's ever pointed that out before…

JAX: (*beat*) Also, because I feel attacked, I should point out that I was referring to an actual female dog, so fuck you, times two. (*snapping back to a pleasant smile*) That was fun. I mean, I was excited to meet with you anyway, but that was just exhilarating, George!

GEORGE: I, uh–

JAX: I should tell you I'm not fucking with you right now. Things are going to get vicious– this is a negotiation, after all. We have to be able to speak freely and (*he closes his eyes, breathes deep, and pushes his arms out as he exhales*) acknowledge and release the tension. Feel free to say whatever you need to say to me, too, George. I mean that.

BEAU: (*meekly*) He does, yeah.

GEORGE: Thank… you?

JAX: (*smiling*) Have I said it's good to see you again?

GEORGE: Uh–

JAX: Since we're all in good spirits, let's dive right in. Loving the storyboards, really, but there is a major concern with the big climax.

GEORGE: Oh?

BEAU: Yes, uh, according to one of our script analysts, there's an alarming number of scenes using tumbling, falling, and heights in some manner. We're concerned–

JAX: The investors are concerned, Beau. We love it. Don't we, Beau?

BEAU: Yes? Yes. The *investors* are concerned...

JAX: ...that we'll upset people with agoraphobia.

BEAU: Are you saying that right?

JAX: Yeah, that's what my notes say. I keep very detailed notes.

Pushing up his sleeve, Jax extends his left arm and squints at his wrist. After a beat, Beau clears his throat gently.

BEAU: My memo says 'acrophobia: fear of heights.'

JAX: Tomayto, tomahto. Point is, we don't want so many scenes with people falling and flipping and every other damned thing. It's unsettling and, frankly, not very believable after the first watch.

GEORGE: These characters don't really fall; they tumble and double jump with their Force powers… think of it more like acrobatics?

JAX: Oh, and it works for the wizards with laser swords. Don't change a thing, there. We want to leave those acrobatics, but trim back in other instances. For example, the investors think you should cut this fifth storyline in your climax where your rabbit-frog Jar-Jar goes into the swamps to fight a boss droid on his own. You've already got enough going on, and that eliminates your literal cliffhanger. If you agree to that, then we're in business!

GEORGE: (*to self*) Cut the fifth storyline… that would streamline a few things… (*to Jax*) Yeah, sure. I mean, I'm sacrificing artistic vision here, but I could make that work.

Jax drums his fingers on the table. He does not speak, just studies George.

Beau lingers quietly in a corner.

GEORGE: Is there something else?

Jax continues drumming his fingers.

JAX: Yeah, but… well, to be honest, I'm still not certain it's an issue. It may just be a 'me' thing, okay?

GEORGE: Uh, yeah, sure. Okay. What, um… what's the–

Seized by dramatic compulsion, Jax smacks the table with both fists.

JAX: There's no *Chew*bacca, George!

George jolts back with a start.

Beau chokes on his bottled water.

GEORGE: Well, uh, no… that's right, there's not.

JAX: Why the fuck not, George?

BEAU: Gotta say, I missed Chewbacca, too. Yeah.

JAX: I think it's a really weak choice. I mean, you've got kid-Vader, kid-Greedo, undergrad Obi-wan and even notes about a shiny Falcon cameo.

GEORGE: How did you like all that?

JAX: I liked it better when I thought we were going to meet teenage mutant ninja Chewbacca in the sewers of your pollution planet or something!

GEORGE: Pollution planet?

BEAU: The dirty city planet that's always gray and gloomy?

GEORGE: That's Coruscant. The entire planet's a city and–

JAX: Nobody cares! You know why?

GEORGE: (*quietly, defeated*) No Chewbacca?

JAX: No Chewbacca! I nearly wept. I do not weep, George. Except for *Schindler's List.* Phenomenal accomplishment. If you don't cry, you're a monster.

George shifts in his chair.

JAX: Here's the thing: the investors ran the numbers, and Chewbacca ticks a lot of boxes in the crowd-pleaser Coliseum. Beau, do you have that printout?

BEAU: Yes, here!

Beau plucks a sheet of paper from a snack counter in the corner of the conference room.

BEAU: According to focus groups, Chewbacca scores higher in onscreen audience appeal than cinema's most popular animal stars.

JAX: I know the significance of this won't be lost on you, George. Like W. C. Fields said, "Never work with children or animals." Those bastards will upstage anyone!

BEAU: In these crowd preference surveys, Chewbacca rates five times higher than toy dogs like Shi-Tzus, three times higher than large dogs like Huskies or Lassie, and– here's the kicker– twice as high as large mammals, like a bear or a lion.

GEORGE: Wow, I… actually, I didn't know that. Can I have a copy of that?

JAX: I'm afraid it's confidential company research. But for the purposes of this meeting, I can let you look at it. Beau?

Beau holds the paper out. George adjusts his glasses, squinting as he reads the numbers.

JAX: Knowing this, just think what a money-maker that goofy Christmas Special would've–

GEORGE: (*loud and upset, like a child*) Strike one!

JAX: What– ?

BEAU: Uh– oh! Jax, you broke his only rule.

JAX: I'm sorry, George. I got carried away with myself. Honestly, I know we aren't supposed to mention… *it*… but you should know that I liked *it* a lot as a kid. Truly.

GEORGE: I'm only counting that as one, but you'd better tread lightly. (*he holds up two fingers, like an umpire*) Two more strikes and I'm out!

BEAU: I think what Jax was trying to express before he derailed himself there is that we wanted Wookies. Instead of Naboo and these weird Gung-hos–

GEORGE: You mean Gungans.

BEAU: Right. Well, instead of them, why not use the Wookies and take us to their home world?

GEORGE: Kashyyk?

BEAU: Sure. If that's what you call it.

GEORGE: I hadn't thought of that.

JAX: Everyone loves Chewbacca, George. He's like the Star Wars sasquatch! Brilliant crowd appeal. I mean that from the heart.

Beau and Jax return to their seats around the conference table. Beau taps his pen, reading off the notes in front of him.

BEAU: Next on the agenda is the racing scene.

JAX: Yes! The pod–chasing stuff! It's great– the setup is great– we loved it, frankly.

BEAU: We did. Yeah.

JAX: But we aren't *in* love with it. Does that make sense?

GEORGE: Um, sure. But, uh... why not?

BEAU: There's concern that fifteen minutes of little pod vehicles zipping around a desert track is going to feel like 'NASCAR in Iraq.' Investors' words, not mine!

GEORGE: Oh, but kids love racing. I see kids at the racetrack all the time.

BEAU: The average attention span for an adult in this country is currently eleven seconds.

JAX: *Seconds*, George. Versus minutes. More minutes than I can count on two hands.

Jax and Beau freeze in position. All the lights dim, save those on George. He looks up, breaking the fourth wall.

GEORGE: (*aside*) At one point in my young life, I deviated from my dream of making a name for myself in racecar circles. I loved the thrill of the chase– watching the road roll away behind me, getting that shot of adrenaline when my fender lined up next to a foe's... man, there was quite a scene for it in California during my younger and more impressionable years... oh, that's good. I should write that down. (*he scribbles a note*) I'm writing about a kid, so I like how that sounded. I'm trying to make Anakin a sympathetic figure, and to do that, I want to see the innocence of his childhood. Uh, Anakin becomes my big bad villain, Darth. Eh, you know. Everyone knows. Except maybe these two idiots. I'm less than amused, but still, I want it! *Need* it! They don't know that. They think I'm just here to get the picture funded. No, I needed notes! Current industry notes from the likes of these peabrains. The same ones who let me keep all my merchandising rights. Short–sighted opportunists. At least their criticism is honest. Everyone else just wants to kiss ass... (*an eerie shift within him*) I have seen other worlds– traveled lightyears in the blink of my mind's eye– and fed it all to you by the shovelful! (*shrugging*) You only live once, I guess... oh, that's good. I should write that down.

George scribbles another note, then turns back to them.

JAX: The investors we have lined up want to keep things current. Three–to–seven–minute scenes, but we're willing to let you drag out some of those laser sword fights if you want.

GEORGE: That feels like it might make the characters a bit... I don't know... two–dimensional, don't you think?

JAX: Please. You've got half a dozen whackadoos with wild–ass names, George. No one's gonna see past the basics. (*in a mocking tone*) "There's the blue sword, the green sword, the princess with antlers and the beeping trashcan with wheels." Nobody's looking for nuance. For instance: you could write every romance scene for this teenager and the nine-year-old in the most stunning poetic verse, and the general public wouldn't know any better. They don't know, they don't care, and they don't care to know.

Just give them something flashy and exciting and, in your case, weird– I mean that as a compliment. The point is, just keep writing about frog–ducks in ponds or whatever the hell that first act was about, and don't go overcomplicating things.

George's face scrunches up; he's strongly considering something.

JAX: Hey, George? You still with us?

GEORGE: Your notes are making me ponder now…

JAX: Good! Care to ponder aloud?

BEAU: Maybe we can be of help?

GEORGE: Well, it's just… all these notes you have on *Phantom*, they're hitting on some insecurities and reservations I have with the project. Part of me wonders what would happen if I just called back Harry, Carrie, and Mark. Are either of you familiar with Mara Jade? From the fiction books based on my movies?

JAX: (*chuckling*) My interns read for me these days, George. It's not something I find 'fun.'

BEAU: I'm more of a *National Geographic* kind of reader.

GEORGE: Okay, so no. Well, she's a brilliant character. The author who invented her did an outstanding job– I hate his guts! Anyway, It's all still mine, right? And I thought, we've got this character already, and she's practically written for me, but what if she goes to the Dark Side somehow? And that's Luke's next salvation mission? Instead of saving his dad, he's trying to save the woman he loves, and she's just completely succumbed to the power of the Dark Side. The Force is what gets between them and their relationship, and, of course, Luke won't want to split up his family. They have a son, Ben, who is also Force-sensitive.

JAX: We could rebrand a whole new trilogy! Star *Divorce.* Really complex, George. I'm with you so far.

BEAU: Really?

JAX: Who can't relate to that?

BEAU: Your target demo, for one. Eight- to twelve-year-old boys aren't going to relate to a divorce story.

JAX: Kids watch their parents go through divorce! That's what I keep thinking these past few months. I keep saying, "Thank God I don't have kids, or Lydia would make this an even bigger mess." I slept in the doghouse one night. In the *actual* dog's house out back. I mean, I tried to sleep in the car, but she locked me out and my keys were still in the house!

BEAU: (*aside to George, overlapping the above*) His wife left him about four months ago. Very sensitive subject.

GEORGE: (*to them both*) That's pretty rough.

JAX: Keep going, George. I like your idea. I think you've got something.

GEORGE: Well, as you know, once the movies were over, Luke went on to re-establish a temple for young padawans. With Leia as part of the New Republic, Luke also has access to people in all the highest places across the galaxy. So, I thought, if he's wrapped up trying to save his wife from the Dark Side, what if she tries to seduce him with his own grasp of power? Because she's loving the things she can do with her powers as a baddie. And Luke keeps going between good and evil, right and wrong. She essentially turns him. She wants the two of them to kill off the Senate and establish their own Empire, with Force-sensitive beings at the top of the new social order. It corrupts everything Luke loves about the Force, but it keeps his relationship pure and intact, and he falls.

JAX: You could even call one of 'em 'The Fall of Skywalker,' or something.

GEORGE: Ooooh, I should write that down!

JAX: See, George, this is what we're talking about! This is the George we were hoping to see. This is-

BEAU: (*reviewing his notes*) It's the Scottish play.

JAX: What?

GEORGE: Huh?

BEAU: Apart from the names, I mean. The formula for this is just the Scottish play.

JAX: You keep saying that like we're supposed to know what it means. What the hell is the Scottish play?

BEAU: It's Shakespeare.

GEORGE: I've definitely never heard of a play called *The Scottish Play* by Shakespeare.

JAX: Yeah, that sounds nothing like a Shakespeare title.

BEAU: It's not the actual name, it's a nickname because you aren't supposed to say the actual title: it's cursed!

GEORGE: Oh, *Macbeth*? Are you talking about *Macbeth*?

BEAU: You're not supposed to say the word!

GEORGE: That's only if you're in a theater! (*the actor may pause to regard the audience before continuing*) And even still, if you are, you can say it if you're in a production of *Macbeth.*

JAX: I hope you're sure because otherwise you just cursed the whole damn office building.

BEAU: Either way, your plot is *Macbeth* and critics are smart enough to see through that.

GEORGE: (*proudly*) I've never read *Macbeth.*

BEAU: Then how do you know so much about it?

GEORGE: (*shrugging*) How do *you*? I thought you said you didn't read anything but *National Geographic.*

BEAU: Film adaptations, obviously.

GEORGE: Oh.

BEAU: The plot device is far too recognizable, George. The wife of a royal is corrupted by power and convinces him they should kill everyone and take over. And you do *not* want to let a critic catch you lifting ideas from any of Shakespeare's best-known works. It's as elementary as three Billie goats about to cross a troll's bridge.

JAX: Shit. He's right, George. I'm sorry.

George tucks those notes back in his bag, shrinking somewhat into his chair as he does.

Beau stands, leaning over awkwardly to show Jax his notes. George sits, waiting patiently.

BEAU: So, um... next note here, Jax. We have... uh... Skid Fist–

GEORGE: Kit Fisto! Oh, he's one of my favorites.

JAX: We can't do it.

GEORGE: (*forlorn*) But why?!

JAX: 'Kid–fister,' George! It sounds like 'kid fister.' Can you really not hear that? Because I can, and that's how I read the damn thing, and it's just not gonna fly! Okay? And don't get me started on the focus groups. I mean, I gotta sell this to kids, George! Christ.

BEAU: He never says that.

JAX: My mother would plotz if she heard me say that.

Jax pushes back from the table, burying his face in his hands. He sits there a moment, then rubs his temples.

GEORGE: Oh, give Kit a chance, Jax. I think kids will love him, really, He's an underwater Jedi–

BEAU: (*to self*) So that's how you say that–

GEORGE: He's an amphibian, so he breathes underwater and uses his laser sword underwater.

BEAU: (*still to self*) I thought it was a soft 'J,' like 'yeti.'

GEORGE: His hair is actually tentacles…. and he's green. Kids love green! Kermit the Frog, Oscar the Grouch... Yoda! I mean, Kit's a real winner. Gonna sell a lot of action figures... a lot.

JAX: (*muttering*) That only helps you, George.

BEAU: What if you simply renamed him?

GEORGE: I'd have to have Lucas Arts reprogram three video games! I'd have to contact Kenner about the action figure! There's a Jedi Temple sleeping bag he was supposed to be on…

JAX: Hold on. George, are you developing merchandise *before* you've found producers for your film?

GEORGE: More like simultaneously.

BEAU: Surely that merch hasn't been printed yet, though. The character's image wouldn't change, just his name.

JAX: Beau's right, George! After all, what's in a name?

GEORGE: Don't get Freudian with me!

Beau shakes his head, his shoulders drooping notably.

GEORGE: 'What's in a name?' Ha! *Everything.* Do you know how long I played with letter combinations to get a name I liked? I spend hours charting these things out, and *months* imagining them as I paint a picture of who they are. That's what goes into a name! You can't just take my name and flip it upside-down. What if I was referencing a beloved film professor or… or a deceased child!

JAX: (*accusatory*) You don't have any dead kids!

GEORGE: You don't know that! This is Hollywood, for fuck's sake! Oh, crackers, now you've got me cursing, too. I really am having a breakdown. Look at me… am I sweating? I feel cold. Oh, God! It could be another panic attack. Oh god, oh god, oh god!

George curls up in a ball on the floor, perhaps hiding under the table.

BEAU: George?

JAX: George! Hey? (*aside*) Whoa! I gave George a panic attack. (*fanning himself*) They're gonna fuckin' fire me for this! If word gets out, I'll be the laughingstock of town. Shit! Shit, shit, shit!

Jax ducks into the corner and snorts a line of coke.

BEAU: Jax?

George rocks on the floor, where he repeats his mantra:

GEORGE: Kit Fisto. Kit Fisto. Kit Fisto…

BEAU: (*a beat*) Okay, everyone, let's reel it in. I think renaming Kit isn't the best idea. Maybe we just keep him in the background, and you can do a cartoon or something later.

GEORGE: Oh, that's great. The tentacles are gonna really sell, I'm tellin' ya'. Studies show kids love tentacles!

Seemingly recovered, Jax stands back up quickly, cocking his head.

Jax: Why? Because of those Japanese cartoons?

Beau buries his face in his hands.

George makes notes on his screenplay pages.

After a beat, Jax stands, tucking his hands behind his back as he stares thoughtfully out a large 'window.'

Beau drums his pencil on the table, regarding George.

BEAU: (*sighing*) You really had something with those first three, George, but... we just aren't sure...

JAX: (*without turning around*) We're not sure you've got it anymore, old man. This script has a lot of problems. The dialogue, for instance– it's so damn whiny!

GEORGE: You said you don't have any kids, is that right?

JAX: That's right.

GEORGE: Take my advice: you wanna know about kids? Go to the action figure section of any retail store, and just wait and listen. It won't take long for you to realize all kids *do* is whine. They're just like critics! Hell, they may even be worse! (*he smacks his script*) They'll totally relate.

BEAU: That's… a fair point, actually.

JAX: Maybe another motion picture isn't the right answer. The script feels so rushed, and clearly you have more ideas than you know what to do with. Have you considered some kind of TV series?

GEORGE: Okay. All right. Now, we're on the same wavelength. I hear you on this. I think I have exactly what you're looking for. Great for kids– music, fun, mayhem. It's about a group of interstellar jazz artists– think *Scooby-Doo* but with a band.

George stands up straight. He clicks a projector on, revealing concept art for The Jizz Wailers.

JAX: *Jizz* Wailers, George– seriously? Is this a joke to you? Fuck off with this nonsense!

Jax and Beau storm out, shaking their heads.

George shrugs, collecting his things. Poignantly, he stops, turns to the audience, and adjusts his glasses.

GEORGE: Everyone's a critic these days…

BLACKOUT

END.

ABOUT THE AUTHOR

Author & entertainer Brent Winzek was born and raised in the hills of Pittsburgh, Pennsylvania. With degrees in film and in theater from Bowling Green State University (Ohio), Winzek spent a decade in New York City working in the Indie Film, Broadway, Off–Broadway, and academic circles of the entertainment industry. After leaving New York, Brent founded Space Cadets Studios, a multimedia & publishing company, to foster the work of like-minded writers and creators. He continues to write & produce strange original work from deep within a forested hovel with his wife and critters.

To explore other projects, visit
spacecadetsstudios.com

ABOUT THE CO-AUTHOR

Writer & performer Zachary Gold was born & raised in Los Angeles, California with his four older brothers. He attained a Bachelor of Arts in Film & Video from The Pennsylvania State University before returning to the west coast to pursue writing. He currently resides in Redondo Beach, California, where he enjoys rock climbing and cooking out when he's not scribbling. Above all, he is grateful for the loving support of his family and friends in all his creative endeavors.

To explore other projects, visit
spacecadetsstudios.com

www.ingramcontent.com/pod-product-compliance
Lightning Source LLC
LaVergne TN
LVHW090613110826
845146LV00001B/376

* 9 7 9 8 9 8 8 5 9 5 5 6 4 *